The Nature Book

The Nature Book

Text and illustrations

Marianne Taylor

Michael O'Mara Books Limited

First published in Great Britain in 2009 by
Michael O'Mara Books Limited
9 Lion Yard
Tremadoc Road
London SW4 7NQ

Papers used by Michael O'Mara Books Limited are natural,
recyclable products made from wood grown in sustainable forests.
The manufacturing processes conform to the environmental
regulations of the country of origin.

A CIP catalogue record for this book is available from the British
Library.

ISBN: 978-1-84317-353-3

1 3 5 7 9 10 8 6 4 2

www.mombooks.com

Cover design by Patrick Knowles Design

Text design and typesetting by K DESIGN, Somerset

Printed and bound in Great Britain by Clays Ltd, St Ives plc

Contents

Acknowledgements

I would like to thank Louise Dixon at Michael O'Mara Books for commissioning me to write this book, Silvia Crompton for handling the editing with efficiency and good humour, Kay Hayden for the elegant text design and Patrick Knowles for the stunning jacket.

Numerous friends and colleagues have chipped in with ideas, suggestions and gentle criticisms during the writing process. A particularly big 'thank you' to Mike Unwin and Graham Taylor for offering their highly contrasting but equally helpful and amusing points of view. My cat Pickle provided timely assistance by moulting helpfully over my keyboard and providing distraction when it was most needed.

Finally, I'd like to thank Rob, as ever, for reading and commenting on bits and pieces of text, bringing tea when required, putting up with late nights and early mornings, saying inspiring and soothing things as appropriate, and generally being brilliant.

Introduction

There's a scene in the arty film *Orlando* in which the eponymous character, disappointed by the opposite sex, rushes out onto a misty moor to a backdrop of sweepingly grandiose piano music, then falls face-down and exclaims passionately through a mouthful of grass: 'Nature, I am your bride! Take me!' If you've ever felt a similar urge to connect more closely with the wilder world but don't know where to start, this is the book for you.

Nature is everywhere. You don't even have to go outside. Whatever you're sitting on right now quite possibly contains bits of what used to be a tree. Maybe there's a plant in the corner of the room, making the most of the carbon dioxide you're exhaling and providing you with some extra oxygen in return. That spider lurking in the corner might make you jump out of your skin but it will be dealing efficiently with any flies that blow in through the open window.

Step into the garden and there's evidence all around you that this world is exuberantly alive. The trees, the small plants, the birds, the insects, the clouds, the wind, the earth: it all fits together on this amazing, dynamic, constantly evolving planet. Look a little more closely at any one part of it and your mind will quickly crowd with questions. Why is that bird singing? Does that cloud mean it's going to rain? What's been eating my cabbages? Why do the leaves fall in autumn? What are wasps for?

You could spend your whole lifetime studying nature and still come away feeling you've only scratched the surface. It's an old truism – the closer you look the more there is to see – but the facts of the natural world are so exhilaratingly diverse, bizarre, comical and shocking that it's time very well spent. This book aims to ease you in gently to this wonderful world by looking at the basics of nature in all its forms, explaining why some things are as they are and hopefully inspiring you to go forth and identify. There is literally a whole world of nature out there.

What's in this book – and what isn't

Beginning with the plant world, we then make our way through the animal kingdom. As well as explaining how both live and develop, this book also gives plenty of examples of interesting things you might see for yourself while out and about in the wilds. It rounds off with a look at our planet as a whole: the way plants and animals interact and form functional ecosystems, the way our weather works, and finally our place in the universe.

Obviously, that's a whole lot of stuff, and some hard decisions were necessary when it came to choosing what would and wouldn't fit in. You're bound to come away with some questions unanswered, and that's where the last section of the book – recommended reading – comes in. The books listed there will provide essential guidance if you'd like to take things a step or two further.

If all goes according to plan, you should come away from this book with your school-biology knowledge refreshed, your awareness of local wildlife improved and your understanding of how it all fits together enhanced. But, most importantly, you should find that your curiosity has been piqued, and your inner naturalist inspired to get outside and start exploring your environment.

We all know that we need nature around us to survive, and that we need to do more to look after it. Of course 'being green' does matter, but pro-green messages all too often work on our guilt; to be honest, they can get rather depressing. What we *don't* hear often enough is that nature is awesome, extraordinary and endlessly fascinating, and will reward your interest with a lifetime of excitement, beauty and revelation.

So be like Orlando and throw yourself headlong on nature's comely bosom. You won't regret it.

FLORA

Trees

WE HUMANS MAY not be as adept as our monkey ancestors at scrambling about in them, but we have retained a healthy respect for, and appreciation of, trees. And with good reason – they shape our landscape, give us our daily oxygen and provide us with food and extremely versatile construction materials. Next time you see one, give it a pat on the back.

A tree begins its life as an embryo enclosed within a seed. The entire seed may be very tiny but nevertheless contains enough stored energy – in the form of a starchy substance called **endosperm** – to sustain the embryo tree while it grows its first roots and shoots. From then the tree sapling starts to collect its own resources from the sun and the soil, and the race is on to grow big and grow fast before it gets eaten or overshadowed. In the tree world, size matters – a lot. You'll probably see a number of little treelets sprouting close to their parent trees when you walk in the woods in early spring, but they are all competing fiercely for any light that isn't already being intercepted by the mature trees, and most of them will lose the battle.

HERE COMES THE SCIENCE PART

Trees function like other plants: they absorb their nutrients and their water from the soil in which their roots are planted, and they make their energy (in the form of a sugar called glucose) in the cells of their leaves by using sunlight to power a reaction between carbon dioxide (CO_2) and water (H_2O). This is **photosynthesis**. The reaction converts the CO_2 and the H_2O into glucose and also some oxygen; the plant stores the glucose and releases the oxygen through the same pores that take in carbon dioxide. In a handy parallel, we animals take in oxygen and produce and exhale carbon dioxide as a side effect of our own cellular energy-making chemistry. This makes for a harmoniously balanced system, gas-wise.

The photosynthesis reaction takes place in **chloroplasts**, tiny bodies inside the cells of a leaf that contain a pigment called **chlorophyll**. This stuff is what gives leaves their green colour and it's also what absorbs the light energy to power photosynthesis. Some trees, like the dark red-brown 'copper' form of the common beech tree, don't have green leaves but they still have chlorophyll; they just have other, stronger pigments as well.

Temperate climates (as distinct from polar and equatorial climates) are good for **deciduous trees** – those that lose their leaves in autumn and remain leafless until the following spring. It's all about energy economy – short, sunless winter days make it inefficient for these trees to maintain a year-round canopy of sunlight-absorbing leaves, while good, high-nutrient soils mean they can afford to grow new leaves each spring. They stop producing chlorophyll in autumn and, as the green pigment disappears, the leaves' other more subtle pigments can be seen, producing all the lovely colours of autumn before they fall. **Evergreen trees** keep making chlorophyll all year round but at a lower level – this strategy tends to work better in more northerly climes and where soil nutrient levels are lower.

What does a tree do all day?

At first, a tree doesn't do much with all that energy and those absorbed nutrients except grow. Within its main stem – its trunk – and all its branches it is constantly adding to the outer layer of wood just under the bark. Across Europe and North America, there is a seasonal pattern in terms of how much new wood is added and when, resulting in the familiar annual growth rings you can see in cut wood.* The wood just inside the bark is very much alive and active, transporting nutrient-filled fluids (aka sap) around – the bark is there to protect this delicate and important new wood from damage. If you make a hole in tree bark, sap will seep out of the wound. If you cut away the bark in a ring all the way around the trunk, the poor tree will die.

As the tree grows and new layers of living wood are added, the wood in the layers underneath dies off. However, it's still an important part of the tree as it has channels for water transport and, more fundamentally, it helps to keep the whole thing standing up.

From treelet to tree

As well as growing upwards, trees generally spread out as well. This makes good sense, as the tree needs to suck up as much sunlight as it can; a big broad umbrella of a canopy helps achieve this. Some conifer trees do things a little differently, forming a Christmas-tree cone shape with the longest

---

* You also get growth rings in salmon. But they're mainly a tree thing.

branches near the bottom, and this design also works well to maximize sunlight-gathering.

Once it's big enough and is generating enough energy, the tree can begin the business of making baby trees. Trees, like other plants, reproduce sexually – by which I mean that male **gametes** they produce (sex cells – in plants they are pollen grains, in animals they are sperm cells) combine with female gametes (or egg cells) to form what becomes an **embryo**, which develops inside a seed. Obviously, trees are too firmly rooted to the spot for any kind of actual copulation to be possible, so the gametes have to find their way to each other by different means.

Shape up: many conifers are cone-shaped, like the Sitka spruce. Scots pines bend the rules and grow in a more conventional shape.

JIM AND ANGIE

Plants come in two basic types according to the way they reproduce – **gymnosperms** and **angiosperms**. In the tree world, the 'jims' are represented by conifers and a few other kinds, and the 'angies' by most deciduous trees (those that shed their leaves in autumn).

'Jims' don't produce flowers, but instead produce male and female cones, the former releasing pollen into the wind, the latter producing female egg cells that will hopefully catch some of that flying pollen and be fertilized. Most of the rest of the pollen will be inhaled by unlucky hay-fever sufferers. Usually each individual tree makes both kinds of cones, but in some species you get exclusively male and female trees.

'Angies' are flowering plants, making pollen and their egg cells inside their flowers. The pollen is made inside projecting **stamens**, the eggs inside a tucked-away ovary that is connected to the outside world via a projecting **stigma**.* In some trees each flower has male and female parts, in others there are separate male and female flowers. Though some still rely on the wind to carry the pollen around, others employ helpers to do it for them, providing a tasty portion of nectar for bees, hover flies and other sugar-loving insects to attract them to the flowers. The insects get covered in pollen from rubbing against the stamens as they feed, which they then carry to the next

* See p.38 for a diagram of a typical 'angie'.

flower and deposit on its stigma, thus fertilizing the flower. Tree flowers vary a lot – some have colourful petals and are easily recognizable as flowers, while others, like the dangly green catkins of willows, are not.

Pass it on

Safely spreading its fertilized seeds to suitable places for germination presents the tree with all kinds of problems. For a start, lots of animals like eating seeds. Many seeds come in some kind of protective casing – the prickly husks of horse chestnut and beech seeds for example – to help discourage this. The idea is that by the time the casing has decayed away the seed has a covering of fallen leaves and is a little safer from seed-munching critters.

If the seed just falls straight down from where it's grown, it will probably be too close to its own parent's shadow to grow successfully. It helps that seeds are ready to fall in autumn when it's often windy, and a good strong gale may help carry them some distance away. Many tree seeds are structured to take advantage of wind power, with 'wings' or clumps of fluff to help them fly further. The 'helicoptering' seeds of sycamores twirl down slowly from the canopy on their blade-shaped wings, their extended airtime increasing their chances of being caught by a passing gust.

Another nifty trick some trees use for spreading seeds around uses animals as unwitting carriers once again. Insects are too small for this job, but it works well with birds and mammals. Such trees produce seeds that are wrapped up inside a capsule of tasty, fleshy, pulpy stuff – what you or I would call a fruit. Let's say it's an apple. The animal eats the apple, enjoying and digesting the pulpy bit. The apple seeds inside survive their journey through the animal's digestive system intact and, by the time that journey reaches its inevitable end and the seeds see daylight again, the animal will have moved a good distance from the parent tree and is hopefully sitting on or above a patch of soil perfect for a brand new apple tree to grow in.*

THE BIRD THAT PLANTS FORESTS

Jays are quite shy and retiring as crows go, which is a pity as they're also very beautiful and colourful. One time when you are likely to see more of them than usual is autumn, when suddenly they're everywhere, flapping purposefully along with (more often than not) an acorn held carefully in their beaks.

A jay on its way to bury – or plant – another acorn

Like many clever animals, jays think ahead; when the autumn bounty of

---

* This is the principle behind the 'fruitarian' diet – eat only what the plant actually wants you to eat. Of course, to do it properly you'd also need to do what bears do, in the woods.

seeds appears, they don't just stuff themselves silly but take the time to put aside an extra supply for the lean winter months ahead. These surplus acorns are buried carefully in the ground; the jay will remember where they are and unearth them as required.

That's the theory, at least. Sometimes the jay will die, or have a memory lapse, or simply not need to retrieve all its stashed goodies, in which case the abandoned acorns have a great chance of successfully germinating, having been taken far away from their parent tree's shadow and buried out of reach of most other acorn-loving creatures. The jay has effectively planted them.

Many an oak woodland has been established by jays, and while it's a risky strategy for the tree, it obviously works well enough, since the acorn itself has no special adaptations to help it to spread or to protect it from being eaten.

Other birds and animals also indulge in this behaviour (hiding food), and in doing so ensure the spread and survival of the very thing they intended to have for lunch.

Berry nice

In autumn, many shrubs and some trees produce eye-catching berries, some of which are distinctive enough to identify the plant. Here are some of the commoner ones you might notice:

- **Blackberry**: Large, round, slightly hairy berries composed of clusters of mini 'berrylets', each of which contains a single seed. They start off red and turn black. The plant is a sprawling, spreading, thorny shrub.

- **Rowan:** Hanging, dense clusters of a few dozen bright-red round berries, which stay on the (usually small) tree into winter.

- **Elder**: Clusters of shiny black berries, more 'structured' and less dangly than rowan berries, growing on a shrub or small tree.

- **Sloe**: The fruit of the blackthorn, sloes are black with a dusty bloom, like miniature plums. The plant is a thorny shrub or small tree.

- **Hawthorn:** Round or slightly oval scarlet berries with the remains of the flower sepals forming a pointy cap at the bottom, growing on a thorny bush or shrub.

TREE TERMINOLOGY

Is it a tree or a shrub? Plants with woody stems are either trees or shrubs – if there is just one main stem (i.e. a trunk) it's a tree, if there are several trunks it's a shrub. Some species, including the yew, can grow as a tree or a shrub. Maybe we should call them trubs, or shrees.

What about bushes and hedges? 'Bush' is just another word for 'shrub'. Stick with 'shrub' if you don't want to spark a political discussion. A hedge is a human creation consisting of shrubs planted close together to make a continuous line – usually as a way of dividing up fields or other areas of land.

What's the difference between simple and complex leaves? If each leaf stem growing out of the twig has a single leaf on it, that's a simple leaf. If the leaf stem has several mini leaves (leaflets – yes, really) growing out of it, that's a complex leaf.

What about the different leaf shapes? Tree field guides will use an array of terminology to describe leaf shapes. Here are a few of the commoner terms:

- **Serrated:** The edge of the leaf has numerous small spikes, like the teeth of a saw, e.g. silver birch.
- **Lobed:** The edge of the leaf may be smooth or serrated, but also has deep indentations – can be rounded or pointy, e.g. oak and sycamore.
- **Pinnate:** A complex leaf whose leaflets are the same size and shape and form pairs along the length of the leaf stem, e.g. ash and rowan.
- **Palmate:** A complex leaf whose leaflets grow from the same point on the leaf stem, are longest in the middle and form a hand shape, e.g. horse chestnut.

The family tree

Most of us can tell the difference between a coniferous tree and a deciduous one, especially in winter. Beyond that, tree identification is a bit more of a challenge but there are two important factors on the would-be tree-identifier's side – trees are generally big or very big, and they don't run away. So take your time and look at as many different aspects of the tree as you can think of. Height, basic shape, bark colour and texture, leaf type (simple or complex), size and shape and the appearance of any flowers, fruits, seeds or cones can all help you pin down what kind of tree it is you're looking at.

A good tree identification book will give you pictures of the whole tree to give an idea of its typical shape, plus close-ups of the leaves, flowers, fruit and maybe the bark. If you don't feel like carrying a field guide around with you but want to learn more about your local trees, take a little notebook out when you go walking and sketch the tree and its leaves/fruit/bark, to check later. If all you want to carry around is this book, the table below should help you identify some of our commoner tree species.

Name	Leaves	Leaf shape	Flower	Fruit	Other
English oak and other oaks	Simple	Lobed; lobes are smoothly rounded	Male green catkins, long-stemmed red female flowers	Acorn: long hard nut in a half-cup	The fresh foliage looks yellowy-green
Common beech	Simple	Oval, smoothly wavy margins	Separate male and female flowers, both round, fluffy and green	Beechmast: small pyramidal nuts in bristly cases	Bark smooth grey, graceful-looking tree

Name	Leaves	Leaf shape	Flower	Fruit	Other
Horse chestnut	Complex	Palmate, each 'palm' comprising five to seven finger-like leaves	Tall spikes of large-petalled white or pink flowers	Conker: large glossy round nut in fleshy case with a few spikes	Leaves appear earlier than most
Scots pine	In pairs	Needles	Cone-like, male flowers yellow, females red	Small with single wings, released from largish oval brown pine cones	Usually has few low branches and a broad canopy
Sycamore	Complex	Lobed; the five lobes have serrated margins and pointed tips	Big hanging clusters of yellow-green flowers	Paired winged seeds	A non-native but now very common tree
Silver birch	Simple	Diamond-shaped with serrated margins	Male catkins long, green and dangly, female catkins small, reddish and erect	Very small, with short double rounded wings	Bark silver-white
Sweet chestnut	Simple	Long and narrow with serrated margins and pointed tip	Male catkins long and green, female flowers small, green and discreet	Chestnut: glossy brown oval nut with pointed tip, in very spiny case	This tree provides the chestnuts we eat
Yew	Simple	Needles	Male flowers green and spherical, female flowers tiny and yellow. There are male and female trees	Cylinder-shaped red berries with a single seed set inside (only found on female trees)	Very, very poisonous and very, very long-lived

Name	Leaves	Leaf shape	Flower	Fruit	Other
Sitka spruce	Simple	Needles	Small and inconspicuous: male flowers are yellow, female flowers reddish	Small, winged seeds released from long, tight pine cones	Christmas-tree-shaped. Not native to Britain but common in plantations
Wych Elm	Simple	Wide and oval with serrated edges and sometimes two extra mini-tips	Clusters of small green and reddish flowers	Small seeds surrounded by round flat wings, which grow in clusters	Since the arrival of Dutch Elm Disease, few live to maturity
Common ash	Complex	Pinnate, with up to fifteen leaflets per stem	Clusters of small brownish flowers	Small seeds with long pointed wings, which grow in clusters	Distinctive black buds in winter
White willow and other willows	Simple	Very long and narrow with smooth margins and pointed tips	Male catkins long and yellow, female catkins long and greenish	Tiny, with tufts of white hairs for wind dispersal	Young willow catkins are greyish and furry, aka 'pussy willow'
London plane	Simple	Lobed, with up to seven pointy triangular lobes	Spherical; male flowers small and green, female flowers larger and red	Spherical and spiny; often there are some on the tree throughout the year	Often has attractive patterned bark
Common Hornbeam	Simple	Oval, longish, serrated edges and prominent veins	Plump yellowish male catkins, female catkins small and discreet	Hard, nut-like fruits with a single long wing, grow in clusters	Round shape, often has very low branches

Name	Leaves	Leaf shape	Flower	Fruit	Other
Rowan or mountain ash	Complex	Pinnate, with up to seventeen leaflets per stem	Big clusters of sweet-smelling white flowers	Bright red berries in clusters	A small tree. Its berries attract birds

The secret world of trees and shrubs

As we've seen, the difference between trees and shrubs is simply the number of trunks they have, and some species can grow as either shrubs or trees. Shrubs may be deciduous or evergreen, very big or very small, but like trees they have thick stems covered in bark, and underneath that is wood. This means that the essential structure of the plant endures the seasons and persists for many years, which makes these plants full-time parts of our environment, unlike the herbaceous plants which die back to the ground (or die completely) at the end of the growing season.

This permanence is one of the reasons that trees and shrubs are really important for other wildlife: they provide shelter and regular food supplies. Lots of birds and mammals can only live in a wooded environment. Many insects take this a stage further and can only live on a particular kind of tree. There are more than 300 kinds of invertebrate animals in Britain that can only feed on the leaves or other parts of English oak trees, and many individuals among them will never leave the branches of the oak tree on which they were born – that one tree is literally their world. There, doesn't that make you feel better about never managing to become an astronaut?

Simple Leaves

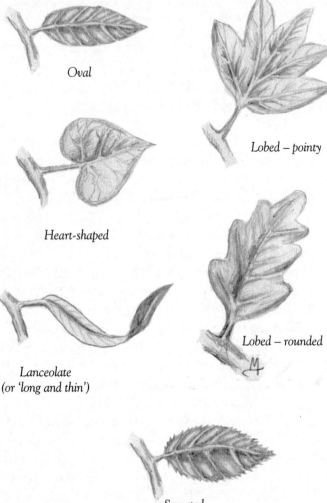

Oval

Lobed – pointy

Heart-shaped

*Lanceolate
(or 'long and thin')*

Lobed – rounded

Serrated

Complex leaves

Palmate

*Pinnate –
opposite-leaved*

*Pinnate –
alternate-leaved*

You'll see these same basic leaf shapes in non-tree plants as well.

Flowers

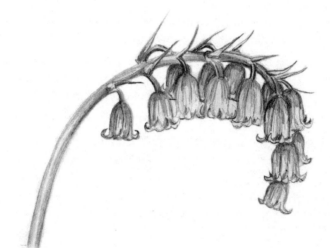

THERE AREN'T MANY statements that could unite humanity in agreement, but surely 'Flowers are pretty' is one of them. We are a species of gardeners, and most of us devote large parts of our gardens not to cultivating useful things such as edible vegetables, but to growing pretty flowers simply because we like looking at them. Out in the wilder world, flowers are the embodiment of nature's beauty... but let's not forget that their sole purpose is to enable plants to have sex.

Some plants live many years, others just for one season. Herbaceous plants (those that have squishy rather than woody stems and die back to the ground at the end of the growing season) are categorized according to how long they survive. They can be annual (living for one year), biennial (living for two years and flowering in their second year) or perennial (living for many years, and usually flowering every year). Spring and summer is the time to make flowers – there is more sunlight so the plant's leaves can make plenty of energy, and it's also the time that insects are on the wing to pollinate the flowers.

COLOUR CODING

Insects visit flowers for nectar and pollinate them in the process. Therefore flower petals need to be bright and showy enough to catch a passing bee's eye. Throughout nature, plants use the whole visible colour spectrum to decorate their petals – and they even create patterns using an ultraviolet spectrum that we humans can't see. Under ultraviolet light we can get some idea of what insects see when they peer into a foxglove or examine an orchid. Plain petals suddenly show strongly contrasting patterning, and patterns visible to us are dramatically enhanced, creating pathways to guide the insects to the nectar. Every flower is effectively a brilliantly glowing advertising beacon, laying out its wares to a discerning clientele of bees, beetles and butterflies.

Flower colours are the result of mixing various pigments inside the cells of the petals. For example, **anthocyanins** produce reds and blues, **carotenoids** make yellows and oranges, **betalains** make reds, violets and yellows, **anthoxanthins** make whites and yellows, and **chlorophyll** – the main pigment in green leaves – makes green colouration in petals, too. Some of these chemicals are mutually exclusive – for example, plants with betalains never have anthocyanins.

All these pigments allow for a dazzling diversity of colour, and horticulturists have developed a wide array of colour combinations and patterns in flowers such as tulips and roses – far more than commonly exist in nature. But wild flowers still have to appeal to insects if they want to reproduce, so they will always have strong ultraviolet patterns, but are less likely to evolve dramatic colour in the spectrum visible to us.

The romance of the rose

Plant reproduction isn't all that different to that of humans and other animals. The male gametes or sex cells – the pollen grains – somehow have to be introduced to the female part of the flower, where they meet and fertilize the female gametes – the eggs. The typical flower is a hermaphrodite, with parts to make male and female gametes, but it doesn't want to fertilize itself if it can avoid it – this is extreme inbreeding and carries a risk of producing unhealthy offspring. It needs to receive pollen from another flower, and it needs to transport its own pollen to another flower, too.*

Some flowers, especially those of trees, distribute their pollen by simply releasing it into the breeze. It's a scattershot approach – a bit like shaking a sackful of pizza menus out of a helicopter window and hoping that some of them get blown into someone's letterbox. Therefore plants that do this have to churn out a huge volume of pollen to be sure some of it will find an appropriate target.

Using a delivery boy (or girl, as is always the case with worker honeybees) to deliver your pizza menus is clearly going to up your chances of success, but you have to pay your workers if you want good results. That's where nectar comes in: flowers produce this sugary treat solely to attract insects. The sweet fragrance that many release is just a hint of the delights to come and is as appealing to insects as it is to us – if you walk on heath land in late summer you'll see bees in their hundreds coming to fragrant heather flowers, while night-scented jasmine and tobacco flowers attract swarms of moths.

CHEATS AND CHEATER-CHEATS

As long as most flowers operate honestly and provide the nectar they're advertising, and the insects fulfil their part of the deal as well, this system will carry on working well, but

---

* Before nature invented sex, everything reproduced by cloning. Combining genes from two individuals introduces more variety and permits faster evolution, as well as being fun.

there's room for a few sneaky individuals to cheat the system on both sides. For example, some bumblebees avoid the tiresome recommended route to a tube-shaped flower's nectar stores and take a shortcut, using their jaws to slice through the petals from the outside. Thus they get the nectar without having to bother with the tedious pollination part.

The flower's counter-manoeuvre is to give every impression of having nectar to offer but then fail to deliver it. Deceived insects do the pollination but get no reward, and the plant gets to hold onto its precious stores of glucose rather than give them up in the form of nectar.

This is an example of an 'evolutionary arms race', where two organisms exert natural-selection pressure on each other. What looks at first glance to be a pleasantly co-operative relationship between insect and flower is actually a tense struggle: each one tries to get away with shirking on the deal in order to preserve its own energy, while at the same time striving to avoid being conned by the other party. Of course, there's no conscious decision-making going on – successful cheaters are rewarded simply by their improved chances of surviving and reproducing.

Too much cheating at once on either side would soon be disastrous for both, though; after all, the insects still need nectar to live and the flowers still need pollination to reproduce. So what we see is the gradual development in both flowers and pollinating insects of more and more elaborate ways to keep each other enslaved.

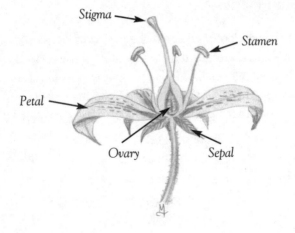

Parts of a flower

The honey trap

Nectar receptacles are situated in such a way that the visiting insect's body comes into contact with the flower's **stamens** (which produce and release the pollen) and its **stigma** or **stigmas** (which catch pollen for delivery to the **ovary**, where the eggs are stored). So in the tubular flower of a foxglove, for example, a portly bumblebee can't avoid brushing against the stamens and stigma on the roof of the flower as it squeezes down the narrow passageway to reach the nectar at the far end. In some flowers, such as snapdragons, the stamens and stigma are tucked away out of sight under a petal, and only pop out when an insect's weight causes the covering petal to give way.

Diversion tactics

So, most flowers look and smell the way they do to attract insects. We can therefore deduce that most of the pollinating insects like sweet smells and pretty colours (oh yes, and those strange ultraviolet patterns). There are some flowers that cater for other insect interests, though – enter the bee orchid.

Hello, gorgeous: a bee about to have a disappointing encounter with a bee orchid

You can see dozens of bee orchid flower-spikes* at suitable places in June, as they like chalky grassland. The plant's flowers look a bit odd, with their round, brown, furry central petals, each with a pair of outspread whiteish petals on either side. The flower's resemblance to a mining-bee might be vague to our eyes, but to a randy male bee it looks – and smells – convincing enough; he heads for the bee orchid in hope not of nectar but nookie. In trying to have his way with the flower, he gets dusted with its pollen, which he then carries to the next flower and so on – a frustrating way to spend a morning.

That's the theory, but it's not a hugely successful strategy compared to the nectar-delivering flowers, and quite a lot of bee orchid flowers end up self-pollinating or failing to form seeds at all, rather ironically. The same goes for fly and spider orchids, which employ the same seduction strategy (for digger wasps and solitary bees, not flies and spiders. Whoever named these two got it wrong).**

Whatever floats your boat

A few flowers appeal to the sordid underclass of insect society – the flies and other scavengers that actually do a valuable cleanup job by eating decaying dead animals and animal poo. The most famous of what are known as 'flesh-flowers' are the rafflesias of Southeast Asia, whose huge, alienesque flowers emit the aroma of rotting meat. Flies and carrion beetles pollinate the giant flowers, whose floppy speckled red petals

* Plants with several flowers on each stem rather than a single one – think orchids v. daisies.
** Just so you know, monkey orchids aren't pollinated by monkeys, and military orchids are not pollinated by soldiers, either.

actually look rather meaty as well. Closer to home are the stink lily and the dead horse arum lily of southern Europe, which sound just delightful, while North Americans can enjoy the unique scent of skunk cabbages. Happily for us, such flowers are very much a minority in the natural world.

The birds v. the bees
Nectar isn't a very important food source for birds in Europe. However, you'll occasionally see warblers or other small birds sporting a telltale yellow dusting on their foreheads, having eaten or tried to eat nectar from flowers. In hotter parts of the world, nectar-feeding birds such as hummingbirds and sunbirds are important pollinators. The former are found in South and Central America and the southern United States, the latter across Africa and southern Asia. Sugar birds, meanwhile, live in southern Africa and mainly eat nectar from protea flowers; flower-peckers are found in Southeast Asia and Australasia; and honey-eaters are mainly Australasian.

Check out the astonishing sword-billed hummingbird, with a bill so long the poor bird has to sit with its head tilted upwards so as not to overbalance and fall off its perch. That bill has evolved in tandem with the ever-lengthening flower tubes of certain passionflowers. At least the hummer knows that no other creature is ever going to get at that nectar... unless they cheat.

After the honeymoon period

Once a flower has been fertilized, those insect-luring petals aren't needed anymore so they wither away and fall off. Now the flower's ovary, formerly discreetly tucked away among the petals, is in full view and begins to swell as the fertilized seed inside ripens. The reproductive process is nearly complete – all that's left is to find a way to spread that seed, and nature has come up with all sorts of ways to do this. Here are the top five.

1. **Just let go**: Annual herbaceous plants naturally avoid the issues perennial plants have about overshadowing or competing with their offspring, so there's no problem just letting the seed fall nearby. Gardeners call it self-seeding.

2. **Take flight**: Windblown seeds can travel long distances – many so-called weeds disperse in this manner. Tiny poppy seeds get blown out of holes in the lids of their seed pods. Dandelion and willowherb seeds have a tuft of fluff to help them glide.

3. **Hitch a lift**: The burdock and the goosegrass produce seeds covered with sticky hairs, designed to catch on the fur of a passing animal and be carried away to pastures new. If no animal passes, the plant can fall back onto option one.

4. **Supper's ready**: Enclose seeds in a tasty fruit. Animal eats the fruit. Animal wanders off and poos the seeds onto the ground far from the parent plant some time later. Seeds germinate. Job done.

5. **You're fired**: The highly invasive Himalayan balsam is one of several plants whose ripe seed pods explode at the slightest touch. The folds of the pod spring open and the seeds shoot out, travelling several metres.

Kinds of flowers

As we saw in the Trees chapter, plants that develop true flowers are called angiosperms, and they comprise the vast majority of plants in the world today, including trees, shrubs and herbaceous plants. Organizing this lot properly into their various taxonomic grouping is, luckily for me, way beyond the scope of this book, but numerous good field guides exist. Here are some of the main flower groups you'll see while out and about:

Daisies are round and usually quite flat flowers with a ring of larger petals around a central core of smaller petals plus stamens and stigmas. The familiar lawn daisy and its scaled-up lookalike the oxeye daisy are among the most instantly recognizable species, but dandelions, cornflowers and thistles belong to the same group.

Orchids have an upright stem bearing several flowers – in some cases the flowers are small and numerous, in others they are large and few. Most orchids are pink or white, and many have very complex petal shapes. The very rare lady's slipper orchid has an astounding bulbous pouch-shaped lower petal, which serves as an insect trap for pollinators. We've already seen what the bee orchid's flowers are like. The man orchid's lower petal is shaped like a tiny person – probably unintentional in this case but you never know with orchids. Ghost orchids are parasites, leaching all their nutrients and energy from other plants. With no need of chlorophyll, they are ghostly white.

Among the most distinctive flower types are the **umbellifers**, which produce lots of tiny, often white flowers on branched and spreading flower heads, a bit like umbrellas. This group includes several species that have been cultivated for food, including fennel and carrot, and others that you definitely wouldn't want to eat, such as hemlock and giant hogweed.*

Common flowers of wasteland, the **pea** family includes all the peas and beans we eat, and some familiar wild plants like gorse and birds'-foot trefoil. Their flowers are two-part, with a projecting rounded lower lip that conceals the stigma and stamens, and a large cup-shaped petal above. Most are yellow or purple.

Capital pea: the broom is a large, shrubby member of the pea family, but its flowers show the same characteristic shape as the much smaller vetches and trefoils

---

* The 1971 Genesis album *Nursery Cryme* includes a very chilling song about giant hogweeds.

Other groups include:

- the **buttercups**, which are flattish with shiny petals and usually yellow

- the **roses**, which may be woody or herbaceous and have open flowers with many stamens and usually pink or yellow petals

- **cabbage**-type flowers such as the cuckooflower, which generally tend to have clusters of four-petalled pink flowers

- the **bell-flowers**, which are usually single blue flowers such as harebells

- the **primrose** family, which includes cowslips and loosestrifes

- the **willowherbs**, which produce tall flower-spikes of many pink flowers

- **sundews**, carnivorous plants that catch insects on their sticky leaves to provide an extra source of protein in their rather nutrient-poor moorland habitat.

And there are many, many more. You'll be needing that field guide.

The plainer relatives

Grasses, sedges, rushes, mosses, liverworts. They're not glamorous so we tend to ignore them (and, in the case of liverworts, wonder what on earth they are anyway). The first three in this list are flowering plants, though, albeit ones that lack big showy flowers (all are wind-pollinated). Grasslands cover a large proportion of the earth's surface – even larger if you include fields of crops like wheat and barley – thriving particularly in places where rainfall is too low to support woodlands. Reeds are a kind of grass that needs a certain dampness – they grow around lakes and rivers, and reed beds form a very important wildlife habitat.

Most rushes and sedges also favour damp habitats. Like grasses they have long, thin, blade-like leaves but their flowers are completely different. Also, their stems are solid (those of grasses are hollow). Sedge stems are triangular in cross-section, while rush stems are round.

Mosses and liverworts are small, simple plants, producing neither flowers nor seeds and reproducing via **spores**. They do still have male and female gametes, though. Liverworts tend to be flattened while most mosses grow more up and out. They form clumps or mats, growing on the ground, on tree branches, on walls and pretty much anything else as long as it doesn't move too fast.

The simplest plants of all are the **algaes**, which include seaweeds as well as single-celled plants that form a vague greenish haze over whatever they grow on, be it wood, rocks or buildings.*

---

* And, in South America, sloths.

SUNNY DELIGHT

The mother of all daisies, the **sunflower** is a plant that all nature-watchers should consider growing in their gardens. It is a fascinating example of flower-kind. As with other daisies, the centre of the 'flower' is in fact a tightly packed mass of small individual flowers (**florets**), each of which will become a single seed. They are arranged in interconnecting spirals in both directions and adhere to a well-known geometrical and mathematical pattern (look up 'golden angle' and 'Fibonacci numbers' if you want to find out more). Typically a sunflower head has thirty-four spirals in one direction and fifty-five in the other. The seeds are immensely popular with seed-eating birds, so if you grow sunflowers, let the seed heads stay in place as they swell and mature and you could attract swarms of greenfinches and their friends.

Fungi

FIRST OFF, LET'S get one thing straight: fungi are not actually plants. We tend to lump them in with plants for one reason: they don't move. Therefore we decide they must be plants and not animals (we conveniently ignore all the many animals – sponges, corals, cats 90 per cent of the time – that don't move either). However, fungi are totally unlike plants in all other respects, and their classification places them in a different kingdom to plants.* That also means that mushrooms aren't vegetables, but luckily for those of us who like eating them they still count towards our five-a-day, for reasons that food standards agencies don't seem to want to reveal.

Finding fungi

You're most likely to notice fungi in the autumn, as this is the time that many of them produce their **fruiting bodies**. These are the familiar mushrooms and toadstools that pop up on the ground or out of rotting wood after rainy nights in October, and are often gone by lunchtime – eaten by animals, kicked out of the ground by passing children, picked by ambitious chefs/would-be poisoners or simply rotted away. Even big, robust toadstools don't usually last more than a few days – the shelf-shaped bracket fungi that grow on trees may last longer. It's not much of a life, but if you remember that the toadstool part equates to the flower on a plant, a reproductive structure only, things start to make much more sense.

The main part of the fungus lives underground, out of sight, and if you dug it up you might not recognize it for what it is. The growing parts of fungi are long, branching structures called **hyphae**, which together form the **mycelium** that comprises the main part of each fungus. The fungal mycelium gets its nutrients by breaking down dead plant and animal tissues and absorbing them, making fungi vital components of the less glamorous end of the food chain. The mycelium looks like a tangle of white fibres – overturn a log in a damp

---

* See p.128 for more on kingdoms and classifications.

woodland and you can see some for yourself, if you really want to. Mycelia can be impressively massive, if nothing else. There is one continuous mycelium of the species *Armillaria bulbosa* under a forest in Oregon which covers thirty-seven acres, is about 1,500 years old and weighs almost 10,000 kg – a humungous fungus indeed and possibly the largest single organism in the world.

Looking for lichens

Lichens, another member of the same family, provide a great natural example of **mutualism**: two living things that function as one and can only survive by living in close association. Every lichen is a composite organism consisting of a fungus and a green **alga** – a simple plant. The fungus part absorbs nutrients from whatever the lichen is growing on, while the alga part photosynthesizes energy in the same way as ordinary plants. Lichens come in a variety of shapes and colours – you're probably familiar with the slightly lumpy, yellowy or orange variety that grows in patches on walls and rocks, and perhaps the crusty pale green kind that covers tree bark. These weird plant-fungus combos are well-known indicators of air quality: lots of lichens mean good, clean air. Visit a forest in the wilds of the Scottish Highlands, Scandinavia or Canada and you'll see just how rampant lichens can be – practically every surface is thickly clad with assorted tufty, leafy or hairy lichens.

MUSHROOMS V. TOADSTOOLS

They're the same thing. We tend to call the ones we eat mushrooms and the scary-looking, wart-covered ones toadstools, and that's a helpful distinction as far as it goes, but the two words have no biological meaning. Nor do they have any meaning to toads, which are unlikely to have a relaxing sit-down on top of any kind of fungal fruiting body.

Sneaky spores

As well as prodigious growth, the fungal world-domination bid is also powered by the distribution of **spores** – effectively single-cell clones of the parent fungus. That's where mushrooms and toadstools come in – they are spore-making structures, and they sprout out of the ground so that the spores they release can be carried off by the wind to new destinations, where they can start to grow a new version of the parent fungus.

Look at the underside of your average mushroom cap closely (wear gloves if it's a wild one and you're not sure whether it's poisonous or not) and you'll see that it has **gills** – narrow strips of flesh – running from where the stalk joins in the centre to the outside edge of the **cap** (a few species have spongy undersides with little holes rather than gills). This is where the spores are made. If you place your mushroom cap gills-down on a piece of paper, cover it up with a bowl and leave it for a couple of hours, you will return to find that your mushroom has left a nice spore-print on the sheet of paper. Spore colours can be helpful in identifying mushrooms.

Dinner or death?

Not all innocuous beige mushrooms are delicious and healthy in a stir-fry, and not all virulently colourful toadstools carry a dose of heart-exploding poison. There are actually more tasty fungi than deadly ones out there, plus a vast middle-ground of those that might give some people an upset tummy, those that induce wild hallucinations and those that have no particular effects on mind or body but taste horrible.

Some are poisonous raw but fine when cooked, while others are OK on their own but not if you wash them down with something alcoholic. Most of us tend to play it ultra-safe and buy our mushrooms from supermarkets – in remoter regions, wild mushrooms are an important and valuable component of many a country dweller's diet and a posh restaurant's menu.*

If you want to start collecting wild mushrooms for eating, your best bet is to go on a 'fungus foray', led by a local expert who will show you what's tasty and what's deadly – and, vitally, how to tell them apart. They will probably advise you to stick to just a few easily identified edible species, while showing you the really nasty species that live in your local area so you know not to eat them.

You'll also need a good fungus field guide, and some gloves. Spore colour, how widely spaced the gills are, what colour the flesh turns if you break a piece off and so on are often more useful for identification than size, shape and colour, so you might need to handle your mushroom a fair bit when

---

* Unfortunately, truffles are rare and grow underground. To find them you'll need a well-trained dog or pig.

identifying it. An open basket is ideal for carrying your haul: not only will you look the part but the mushrooms will remain in good condition – they'll quickly turn into slimeballs in a plastic bag.

Five to avoid

1. **Fly agaric**: The classic 'poisonous toadstool' of the darker brand of fairytale, it's the big red one with white warty spots. It (probably) won't actually kill you but can make you very sick.

2. **Panther cap**: Related to the fly agaric, it's brown with white spots and is much more poisonous.

3. **Death cap**: This one has a smooth, grey-green cap, is otherwise white and has a **volva** – a distinctive bag-like structure around the base of its stem. Very, very poisonous.

4. **Destroying angel**: The names get better and better... This is a pretty, pure white and ferociously poisonous mushroom, related to the Death Cap and also possessing a volva.

5. **Deadly webcap**: A dark red-brown mushroom with well spaced gills and, when young, a cobweb-like veil connecting the cap to the stem. Unsurprisingly, it's deadly.

SHAMANIC SHENANIGANS

The striking fly agaric fungus has an array of distressing effects on the human nervous system if eaten, including inducing wild hallucinations. Siberian shamans have long used fly agarics to send them into trances, wherein they communicate with the spirit world and (if they recover) convey their findings to the rest of the tribe. It has been suggested (though not widely believed) that the modern image of Santa Claus, dressed in red and white just like the mushroom and accompanied by flying reindeer, could be derived from fly agaric hallucinations.*

Five to enjoy

1. **Field mushroom**: Related to commercially grown mushrooms. Whiteish with pink to dark-brown gills, and a ring around its stem.

2. **Horse mushroom**: Big brother of the field mushroom – similar in all respects but larger and tastier, though sadly less common.

3. **Cep**, **porcini** or **penny bun**: The classic lovely wild mushroom – it has a domed, bun-like brown cap, white stem and no gills. It has many lookalike relatives, some equally tasty, others not.

---

* Best not tell the kids this just yet.

4. **Giant puffball**: Looks like a big white ball with no discernible stem. Get it young while the inside is solid white, before it becomes a mass of spores – cut it in half to check you don't have an immature cap-type fungus.

5. **Chicken-of-the-woods**: Another great descriptive name. A yellow bracket fungus, growing in closely packed shelves on (usually) damaged oak trees, it's around from spring so is an out-of-season fungal treat.

Five to puzzle over

1. **Stinkhorn**: Tactfully named for its bad smell, but you're more likely to notice its unusual shape. Its scientific name is *Phallus impudicus* – 'nuff said.

2. **Shaggy inkcap**: A parasol-shaped mushroom, its ragged fringes turn black and drip away as it matures.

Puffed out: earthstars release puffs of spores when raindrops fall on them, or when they are poked by curious passers-by

3. **Earthstar**: Like a fancy puffball, this fungus has a central ball set in a many-pointed star of folded-out edges, like a very neatly peeled orange.

4. **Morel**: The various different kinds of morels have stout white stalks bearing a contrastingly coloured bulbous head of honeycomb-like pits and ridges.

5. **Yellow brain fungus**: This alarming-looking fungus sprouts out of dead wood, and looks like a bright butter-yellow, convoluted blob of jelly.

FAUNA

Mammals

GOT MILK? Then you're a mammal. You're also warm-blooded, probably have a selection of teeth of different shapes and sizes and are somewhat hairy or furry, but it's the presence of mammary glands that makes mammals unique. No wonder we celebrate this special attribute so prominently on page three of our favourite tabloid newspapers.

Mammals and birds are both warm-blooded, or **endothermic**, which means they can maintain a consistent internal body temperature by various mechanisms including shivering and burning up body fat to warm up, and cooling down by panting, flushing (bringing blood close to the surface of the skin) and sweating. They both evolved from reptiles, but while the front legs of the protobirds became wings and their jaws became bills, the majority of mammals retain a much more reptile-like body plan with four walking limbs, a tail and jaws full of teeth.

We think of mammals as the most advanced and successful animal group, probably out of a sense of familial pride. We're wrong, though. With only 5,400 species, mammals lag behind fish, birds, reptiles and amphibians in terms of diversity – and almost half of that 5,400 is made up of rodents. Without all those rats, mice, voles and squirrels, the mammalian contribution to life on earth looks positively pathetic. Still, the group does include the most influential species of them all: us.

Meet the relatives

There are some thirty main groups of mammals. Some are very familiar to us, others much less so. Here is a representative sample:

Primates: That's you and me, plus the other great apes, all the monkeys and a motley crew of monkey-like relatives including lemurs, bushbabies, lorises, tarsiers and a host of other wide-eyed, fluffy, tree-climbing creatures. Primates have hands, big brains and are mostly forest-dwelling vegetarians.

Carnivores: Lions and tigers and bears (oh my!). And dogs, foxes, weasels, raccoons, civets, mongooses and even seals. If it has pointy fangs and is mainly a flesh-eater, it probably belongs here.

Ungulates: Animals with hooves. Often big and always herbivorous. The ones with an even number of toes and the classic split-hoof footprint – deer, cows, antelopes, sheep, pigs, camels – are not actually closely related to the odd-toes (that's horses and their allies, tapirs and rhinos).

Rodents: The gnawers, with big, blunt incisor teeth for chewing through tough plant material. Rats, mice, voles, squirrels, beavers, coypus, hamsters and guinea pigs all belong here, but rabbits and hares don't – they're in a different group called the **lagomorphs**. Most rodents are small or very small.

Cetaceans: These are the whales, dolphins and porpoises – the most aquatic of all mammals. They have no hind limbs and are essentially fish-shaped, but they still have to breathe air, using blowholes on the tops of their heads.

Bats: To show there's nothing mammals can't do, this group has conquered the skies. Their front limbs are wings, the long fingers joined by leathery membranes. Some bats are small and insectivorous, the rest are bigger and eat fruit.

Pipsqueak: like other bats, pipistrelles squeak constantly as they fly, using the echoes from their squeaks to build a 'sound map' of their surroundings

Marsupials: The most primitive of mammals and mainly restricted to Australasia, this is a diverse group including predators, nectar-feeders, grazing animals and insect-eaters. All female marsupials have a pouch, into which their tiny, almost embryonic babies crawl after birth.

Other mammal groups include insectivores (moles, shrews and hedgehogs), the 'pilosids' (anteaters and sloths), the egg-laying mammals or monotremes (platypuses and echidnas) and several odd-bods including elephants, manatees and hyraxes. So while we lag behind the birds in terms of number of species, we mammals have a much wider variety of lifestyles than our feathered friends.

Mammals in Britain

We have a slightly lame selection of mammals in the British Isles these days. Once upon a time, there were brown bears, wolves and lynxes, but our ancestors wiped them out. Now our most fearsome predator is the fox or maybe the grey seal. The only hoofed mammals native to Britain are a few kinds of deer; no sweeping herds of wildebeests across the plains or big cats skulking in the forests for us. The mammals we do have include some wonderful – albeit smallish – creatures, however, and because there aren't too many of them, we can take a proper look at them.

Rodents

British rodent fauna contains rats and house mice, which most of us would cross the street to avoid, and the controversial non-native grey squirrel (aka 'tree rat'), which attracts affection and loathing in equal measures. But we also have cuties like dormice, water voles and (in Scotland, Ireland and a few parts of England and Wales) enchanting red squirrels. Most rodents are nocturnal, and some hibernate through winter, so seeing them means early starts and a lot of luck.

Shrews and shrewish creatures

There are four kinds of shrew in Britain, all ravenously hungry little beasties with insanely high metabolisms. They get through almost their whole bodyweight of food a day in the form of insects, snails, centipedes and other invertebrates, and are so dedicated to the pursuit of the next meal that they will rush right past you as you sit in the grass having a picnic. You'll often find dead ones lying on pathways – perhaps they starved to death before they made it across the path. The mole is closely related to shrews and you'll have seen its molehills if not the velvety little animal itself. Hedgehogs are easier to see – put out dog food for them if they visit your garden and you could enjoy hours of happy night-time pincushion-watching.*

Hunter-gatherers

Most of the British carnivores belong to the weasel family. Weasels, stoats, minks, polecats and pine martens are pretty similar – elongated animals with little round ears, bright eyes, shortish legs, longish tails and a rippling way of moving. All are incredibly fearless hunters. You could, with lots of luck, witness a stoat tackling a rabbit almost anywhere in Britain; the little hunter doesn't hesitate to chase down and pile onto

---

* Not bread and milk. It gives them the runs.

David and Goliath: dwarfed by its rabbit prey, this triumphant stoat will dine well today

the much larger bunny. Minks (which are non-native, descending from fur-farm escapees) are often seen swimming in rivers. Otters are much bigger and browner, and your best bet for seeing them is the seas around Scotland. Pine martens live in northern forests and moorlands, and if you live in a pine marten area you may be able to tempt them to your garden by leaving out tasty snacks – peanut butter smeared on fence posts is a favourite.

Cats large and small

Britain may have lost its lynxes but still has a formidable wild feline living in remote Caledonian forests: the Scottish wildcat. Unfortunately, this very rare animal looks much like a domestic tabby, even though the two are different species (or subspecies, depending who you listen to). Even the cats themselves don't seem to be able to tell the difference, and

WEASELLY RECOGNIZED, STOATALLY DIFFERENT

Was it a stoat or a weasel? You probably saw just a bounding brown streak, but even with terrible views it's still often possible to tell one from t'other – here are the key features to look for:

- **Size**: Stoats can be considerably longer, and look more substantial. Weasels look like pumped-up, stretched-out mice.

- **Tail tip**: The stoat tail has a black tip, while the weasel's is all brown.

- **Pattern**: Both are brown on top with white tummies, but in the stoat the line between brown and white is neat, in the weasel it's wobbly and untidier.

- **Colour change**: Most stoats turn white or partly white in winter (save the black tail tip). Weasels don't.

Don't give up on seeing your steasel or woat properly even if it's disappeared into the long grass. Stay still and make soft squeaky noises – you might sound enough like a giant mouse to pique the critter's curiosity and entice it back for a second look.

our Scottish wildcat population is being slowly but surely copulated out of existence by feral or roaming domestic cats, its genetic uniqueness disappearing. The wildcat is probably the most difficult of all our mammals to see but you might get lucky while wandering far off the beaten track in the Scottish highlands.

Sociable types

Badgers and foxes are Britain's biggest land carnivores, and both live in burrows in the woodland so are often lumped together. They're very different animals, though. The badger is a weasel-relative, and an intensely sociable animal. You'll know a badger sett when you see it – there will be many big holes close to each other, some of them surrounded by piles of recently thrown-out earth. Badgers are incredibly sensitive to dodgy smells, including that of people, so don't loiter round the sett at dusk as the badgers will probably stay at home and patiently wait for you to leave. There are organized badger-watching places in Britain, and many people have badgers visiting the garden – they like cat or dog food, peanuts, jam sandwiches and fruit if you want to feed them.*

FOX CLEVER

How come there is still an abundance of foxes when so many other native predators are rare, very rare or extinct? It's not as if we humans have been any nicer to our foxes than we were to lynxes, bears and wolves. It's only been a few years since hunting was banned and foxes are still being killed – legally and illegally – all the time throughout Britain.

---

* They'll probably dig up your garden a bit. But no self-respecting wildlife enthusiast has a pristine garden anyway.

Foxes are special, that's why. They belong to that select group of animals that has what it takes to succeed in a country dominated by humans. Like street pigeons, crows and rats, foxes are clever, enterprising and adaptable. They will eat almost anything and live almost anywhere. Urban foxes are everywhere now – take a drive by night through many an English town and you'll see plenty of bushy-tailed marauders looking for a bin to overturn. You may even have seen a litter of cubs frolicking in your garden – and it would take an exceptionally stern heart not to be melted by that.

The issue of foxes harming farmers' livelihoods is a vexed one. Foxes are unlikely to attack lambs, though they might try their luck with an undersized or feeble one. They certainly will go for chickens and other poultry, but so will any stoat or buzzard worth its salt. In any case, the fox has so far coped in style with all the horrors we've thrown at it over the centuries. That surely makes it worthy of our admiration and respect.

Big ears

There are three species of rabbits and hares in Britain. If you're wondering what the third one is you must be a southern softie – besides the familiar rabbit and not-quite-so-familiar brown hare, we also have mountain or Arctic hares: pretty, grey, bunny-shaped animals of the moors and mountains that turn white in winter save their black ear tips.

There's a deer

The two native deer species in Britain – the red and the roe – have been joined over the years by several non-natives, some introduced on purpose and others by mistake – the fallow, sika, muntjac and Chinese water deer. The red deer stag is the biggest, the original Monarch of the Glen with its fine spreading antlers and shaggy neck. The muntjac is the littlest one, no bigger than a medium-sized dog and shy with it.

DEER, OH DEER

Seen a deer? Don't know what kind it is? Pay attention to the following points: size, antler shape (if it's a male), coat pattern, and what the tail and backside look like. Then consult this table:

Species	Red deer
Size	Very big, up to 140cm at the shoulder
Antler shape	Spreading and branch-like with many pointy tips
Coat pattern	Solid brown, redder in summer, greyer in winter
Tail/bum	Short tail, bum has narrow white patches

Species	Fallow deer
Size	Medium-sized, up to 95cm at the shoulder
Antler shape	Spreading, very broad and flattened
Coat pattern	Plain brown in winter, brown with white spots in summer (but very variable)
Tail/bum	Long, black, centred tail, narrow white bum patches outlined with dark horseshoe

Deer headgear – who wears what?

Roe deer

Muntjac

Red deer

Sika deer

Fallow deer

Species	Roe deer
Size	Smallish, up to 75cm at the shoulder
Antler shape	Small, quite straight with few points
Coat pattern	Solid brown, very russet in summer
Tail/bum	Tail barely noticeable, big round white bum patch

Species	Sika deer
Size	Medium-sized, up to 95cm at the shoulder
Antler shape	Spreading and branch-like, smaller than those of red deer
Coat pattern	Plain grey-brown in winter, dark brown with white spots in summer
Tail/bum	Tail white, bum patch heart-shaped and white. Note also round pale scent gland on hind legs

Species	Chinese water deer
Size	Small, up to 55cm at the shoulder
Antler shape	None, though male grows large prominent tusks that poke down like fangs
Coat pattern	Plain light grey-brown, more sandy in summer
Tail/bum	Tail barely noticeable. Bum the same colour as the rest of the deer, no white patches

Species	Muntjac
Size	Very small, up to 50cm at the shoulder
Antler shape	Short, straight with no branches, i.e. only one point
Coat pattern	Reddish brown with dark line down centre of face continuing right down the back
Tail/bum	Longish tail, held up when running away. No white bum patches

Batty about bats

There are lots of kinds of bats in Britain. The ones you're most likely to meet are the noctule, a big and slowly flapping bat, and the pipistrelle, a tiny fluttery creature with an inaudibly high squeak. Close examinations of the pipistrelle's squeak has led bat-scientists to conclude that there are actually three different species of British 'pip'. That's neither here nor there to most of us, as they all look the same in the dark, and indeed in daylight. If you're very keen on bats, though, you could invest in a bat detector, a handy gadget that will analyze the squeaks and identify the bat for you.*

Offshore assets

Finally, there are the sea mammals. Two seals breed around our coast – the **grey** and the **common**. To tell them apart, check out the profiles. The grey has a distinguished Roman nose, while the common has a distinct concave dip between forehead and snout, giving it a more dog-like face. Boat trips off the Norfolk and Suffolk coast are great ways to get up close and personal with colonies of seals, of both kinds.

Seal the deal: both grey and common seals are grey, and grey seals are commoner than common seals. So forget all that and look at its profile. Forehead dip and pronounced muzzle = common; Roman nose = grey.

---

* Bats enjoy extremely strict legal protection from harassment. Don't ever disturb them at their roosts, and don't call them rude names.

A WHALE OF A TIME

Britain is extremely good for whale- and dolphin-watching, easily matching world-famous destinations. No, really. You don't have to go to South Africa or Iceland to see orcas, bottlenose dolphins, fin whales and many more. Headlands on the coasts of Scotland and south-west England are particularly good places to sit and scan the waves, but better still is to take a boat trip out into deeper water. You could then see common dolphins bow-riding alongside you, almost close enough to touch, watch minke whales spouting and rolling as they feed, and see harbour porpoises lying asleep on the surface, one fin stuck casually in the air.

The best trips of all are the ferry crossings that go through the Bay of Biscay. The deep waters here attract many whales and dolphins (and seabirds) – such delights as blue and humpback whales, Cuvier's beaked whales and Risso's dolphins are regularly seen on the way to Santander or Bilbao. So if you're looking for an excuse to take a slow boat to Spain, this is it.

A mammal's life

Mammals are mostly very private creatures. On the average country walk you might see rabbits and grey squirrels, but probably no others unless you're very lucky or very patient. Mammals have keen noses and as long as there's a breeze blowing from you to them they will know when you're coming however long you spent in the shower that morning. Most of them are nocturnal as well, which doesn't help.

Small mammals live hard and die young. Most mice and voles will keel over from old age before they've lived two years, if a predator doesn't get them first, and those short months of life are packed with parenting. A long-lived and very fecund female house mouse could produce fifteen litters in her lifetime, irrespective of season. Bigger mammals live longer, though mammals in general aren't as long-lived as birds, and most species follow a lifestyle that fits in with the rhythm of our seasons.

Family planning

Female mammals typically have a receptive time when they can become pregnant. With foxes, this is in winter, with red deer it's autumn, with mice it's every three or four days from the age of six weeks. Receptive females usually means extremely hyped-up males, and some famous and fascinating mammal behaviour.

You can see deer rutting in deer parks such as Richmond Park in London, Knole Park in Kent, Powys Castle in Wales and many other places. Wild deer are more elusive, but the Scottish moors have large numbers of red deer, while lowland woods in southern England are good for fallow deer. The rut entails male deer competing to impress the females. A successful male attracts a large harem of females, and must spend his time alternately mating with all of them, rounding them up so they don't stray from his side, and doing battle with rival males. No wonder the stags lose some 14 per cent of their body weight over the rutting weeks. The battles usually consist of posturing and shouting contests, but if two males believe they are closely matched based on their roars, a physical fight may ensue, with the males loudly clashing antlers and shoving each other around. A serious fight can result in injury or even death for the loser.

Stoats mate in late summer, but the fertilized eggs don't actually implant (i.e. form a placenta and begin to develop) until the next spring, they just bob about inside the uterus in a state of suspended animation until the lengthening spring days trigger something in the stoaty brain and the process begins. Why this occurs is a mystery. One theory is that the young female stoat can get mating out of the way and then spend all winter organizing a nice productive territory for herself and a den in which to have her babies. Its little cousin the weasel does not do the delayed implantation trick but gives birth five weeks after mating in spring, possibly because it doesn't live as long as the stoat and can breed twice a year. Neither stoat males nor weasel males help rear the young, but spend all their time from spring to autumn looking for new receptive females to mate with.

MARCH MADNESS

They're a lot rarer than rabbits, but you could still see brown hares in grassy areas throughout most of Britain. They're much leggier than bunnies, with staring, somewhat unhinged-looking amber eyes and long, black-tipped ears. If you know where to see hares close to you, make sure you go looking for them in March to see the spectacle of their courtship behaviour.

The females are on heat at this time, and the males are frantically attempting to mate with them. This means breathtaking high-speed chases across the fields, and boxing matches where two hares face off, rear up on their hind feet and whack at each other with furious paddling movements of their forepaws. The boxing pair are not rival males but an over-amorous male and a disinterested female trying to fend him off. Some males won't take no for an answer and both parties can end up getting cuffed in the face. It's all over by mid spring and the females give birth to their babies – leverets – a few weeks later. The leverets are much better developed than young rabbits and can hop about soon after birth.

Gerroff: a female hare prepares to thump
an overenthusiastic admirer

Bats mate in the autumn, the males attracting the females' attention within the colony with special squeaks and smells. Males sometimes actually copulate with females after the latter have already begun their hibernation. Implantation is delayed until spring in some species, while in others fertilization itself is delayed and the male's sperm lives inside the female's uterus all through winter, until she ovulates in the spring.

Bouncing babies

Baby mammals all feed on their mother's milk. This means that males are often quite unnecessary for child-rearing, and so proper pair bonds in mammals are quite rare. Sometimes several females are guarded by one male, who helps to protect the females from danger and unwanted sexual advances. In other species, the female goes it alone, feeding her babies herself and handling their tricky transition from dependent infants to self-sufficient adolescents.

Bats give birth to unusually large and well-developed babies, about a quarter the weight of the mother (imagine a 30lb-plus human newborn, and wince). That way, their vulnerable flightless stage is very brief, and baby bats are flying about when they're just three or four weeks old. Since the female bat cares for her babies alone, keeping the childcare period to a minimum is essential if she is to emerge relatively unscathed from the experience.

Foxes are something of an exception in the mammal world, with pairs usually sticking together long-term (once the noisy winter courtship period is over) and co-operating to rear their cubs. The male's job is to bring food to the female while she is heavily pregnant and subsequently feeding the new cubs. Sometimes, they practise **polygamy**, whereby one female and her babies are looked after by two or more males, or one male looks after two or more females and their litters. The former arrangement is more likely to occur when food is thin on the ground, while in times of plenty the latter makes more sense.*

In badgers, usually only the dominant pair in the group breeds. Mating may happen at any time of year, but the females use delayed implantation, enabling them to time the birth of their cubs to coincide with the best foraging conditions. The cubs are out and about after about six weeks, leaving the sett at dusk to forage with the rest of the group and gradually extending the range that they'll explore every night. They are self-sufficient within about four months. In midsummer, if you go out in the woods very early in the morning you could bump into a badger group with little ones in tow, hurrying home for their daytime sleep.

Baby names

There's lots of confusion and disagreement over what the babies of various animals should be called. Here's a look at the most popular names:

badgers	cubs
foxes	cubs or kits
weasels and their relatives	kits
seals	pups
whales and dolphins	calves

---

* Polygamy works both ways. If you want to get specific, **polygyny** means one male, several females, The other way round is **polyandry**.

rats, mice, shrews and their ilk	pups or kits
rabbits	kits
bats	pups
hares	leverets
hedgehogs	hoglets
wildcats	kittens
large deer	calves
small deer	fawns

And a few more, some more widely accepted than others:

goats	kids
sheep	lambs
horses/zebras	foals
antelopes	calves
wolves	cubs
big cats	cubs
small cats	kittens
platypuses	platypups, puggles
kangaroos	joeys

Watching mammals

While lots of us go out bird-watching now and then, and can be pretty certain of coming home having actually seen some birds, mammal-watching is very different. Most mammals are shy, paranoid, hypersensitive and come out mainly at night, so you need special care and preparation to boost your chances of seeing them.

Follow the clues

To find out which mammals are around in your local area, look out for the signs they leave behind. Rodents leave behind the chewed-open shells of nuts, often in characteristic patterns. If you find a pile of bird feathers, check the state of them to figure out what killed the bird – if some of them have been bitten through, it was probably the work of a fox. Badgers are the only animals which can tackle rolled-up hedgehogs, prising the poor hog open with their big claws and then eating the squishy parts, leaving only a hollowed out spiny skin behind. Hares leave shallow depressions of flattened grass from where they've been lying down. Holes dug into riverbanks are the work of water voles. Tree foliage eaten away from the ground to deer-height is a sign of… deer. All mammals (well, maybe not bats or whales) leave tracks on suitable ground – mud, sand and snow are all good.

Stealth and timing

Now you know which mammals live near you, it's time to try to see them. In general, summer is a good time to look, thanks to the shorter nights. Go to your target place before dawn. Move quietly and invest in a coat that doesn't rustle. Try to look inconspicuous – you don't have to fasten mud and branches to your person but wearing dull colours is a good idea. Approach downwind of your intended spot, find a good hiding place and prepare for a long wait. If you have the basic primate skill of tree-climbing, waiting up a tree can give you a better chance of seeing non-climbing animals like deer and badgers. If you are waiting at a badger sett or another animal burrow, don't wait too close or you'll freak them out.

Who goes there? Some common mammal paw prints

Grey squirrel
(front foot – the back has five toes)

Mouse or vole

Badger

Hedgehog

Rabbit (this shows all four paw
prints of a resting bunny – the paws
are too furry to leave pad prints)

Fox

Stoat

Otter

Red deer

Roe deer

Fact or fiction?

We love our ancient and modern mythology, and there are plenty of suppositions and superstitions concerning mammals. Here are a few of them.

Are there really black panthers and other big cats roaming Bodmin Moor and elsewhere? Probably yes, from time to time. Unwise people have always found ways to keep impressive wildlife as pets, even though it's very illegal to do so without the proper premises and licensing, and when a puma or leopard turns from cute cub to unmanageably powerful and hungry adult, it may well end up being released into the wild. Having said that, most photos of ABCs (alien big cats) actually show domestic cats from funny perspectives. And there's no such thing as a black puma, so a big black wild cat will be a black leopard (panther) or a black jaguar. If you see one, don't panic as it will probably want to run away rather than eat you.

Are you really never more than six feet away from a rat? It depends where you are of course but no, even in grimy urban hell you're often much further from your nearest rat. A very detailed study in New York revealed a rat:human ratio of 1:36, not the oft-quoted but wholly inaccurate 1:1.

Do foxes kill for pleasure? Anyone who's had the misfortune to see what a fox will do if it gets into a henhouse will probably say yes, because there's no way one fox could eat all those chickens. Well, it couldn't eat them all in one go, that's true. But foxes are prey-stashers – if they get lucky and find a glut of prey they will kill all they can, eat their fill and hide and bury the rest for a rainy day. It's nothing to do with psychotic blood lust and everything to do with forward planning. They probably won't have time to go back for every last chicken in the henhouse before the crime is discovered, though.

Is the grey squirrel responsible for the red squirrel's decline? The evidence all points to 'yes'. Grey squirrels use the same habitats as the reds, but they are bigger and stronger, so simply out-compete the reds and use up all the resources for themselves. There's more, though – grey squirrels carry a particularly horrible disease called parapox, to which they themselves have developed antibodies so it doesn't kill them. It does kill the reds though, so whenever red and grey meet, parapox can enter the red squirrel population. Therefore, conservationists are doing all they can to stop the greys spreading further north to the Scottish strongholds of the reds.

Birds

Y OU'LL PROBABLY NOTICE more birds than any other kind
of wildlife while you're out and about. Mammals are too
shy, reptiles and amphibians are hiding under things and
insects are mostly too small. But birds, with their power of
flight, can flaunt themselves in front of us to a greater extent.
That's why there are so many more bird-watchers out there
than there are worm-spotters or wasp enthusiasts.

WHAT MAKES BIRDS UNIQUE?

Flight? No, insects and bats can do that.

Laying eggs? No, lots of animals do that including fish, many insects and even snails and slugs.

Being warm-blooded? No, mammals are, too.

Having feathers? Aha! No other group of animals has these. Feathers come in various different shapes, each of which has its own function. The big strong ones in the wings and tail help the bird fly and steer. The tiny fluffy ones close to the body keep it warm. Finally the main body feathers form the canvas for the bird's dazzling – or dull and camouflaged – colours.

Is it a bird?

As well as their unique feathers, all birds have two wings, two legs and a beak (or bill).* For most birds, the wings are for flying, the legs for walking about or perching, and the bill for grabbing food. Look at some of the birds you know well and you'll notice differences in the way their bodies are shaped – these all tie up with differences in their lifestyles.

---

* City-dwellers familiar with street pigeons may dispute this leg-count.

Some bird bill and foot shapes

Peregrine falcon

Garganey

Ring-necked parakeet

Dunlin

Goldfinch

Grey heron

Next time you see a duck out of water, look at its feet. The toes are joined by thick webbing, giving the duck a pair of big paddles for powering along through the water. A gull has these webbed feet, too, but its feet are much smaller – it's not as good a swimmer as the duck. However, its legs are much longer, making it better at running about on dry land than the duck is. The duck has a flat, wide bill for dabbling in the water. The gull's bill is pointy – no good for dabbling but great for snapping. The duck's short, pointy wings mean it has to work hard to get airborne but once up can go very fast. The gull has longer wings, which means it can glide, soar and hover, but it isn't that fast. By looking at a bird's bill, feet and wings, we can usually tell roughly what kind of bird it is and how it goes about its lifestyle.

The main types of birds

All the birds in the world (and there are about 10,000 species of them) belong to one of about thirty main groups. Here are some of the more familiar groups, and the features shared by the birds belonging to them:

Penguins: Everyone's favourites. Black-and-white, flightless, they walk on land with an engaging waddle but swim swiftly and elegantly using their flipper-like wings. Some live in Antarctica, but many don't.*

---

* If you see a penguin on Brighton or Blackpool beach, it isn't one. It'll be an auk.

Waterfowl: Ducks, geese and swans. Big birds with webbed feet, flattened bills and a fondness for water. Most swans are white, most geese are grey or brown, and in most ducks the male is colourful while the female is drab.

Game birds: Pheasants, partridges, grouse, chickens, turkeys. Stocky, plump vegetarian land birds. Often the males are big and colourful, the females smaller and dingier. They have strong legs for walking and running, which they much prefer to flying. We like eating them, which is possibly why many species are extremely shy and live in very dense forests.

Birds of prey: Hawks, falcons, eagles, buzzards and the like. They mostly catch mammals or other birds, and are equipped with hooked bills and talons to help them grab and kill their prey. Most are agile fliers, able to go very fast or glide for long spells – or both. Often the females are larger than the males.

Waders and gulls: This is a mixed bag of birds, including plovers, sandpipers, gulls, terns, skuas and auks.* They are mostly sea or coastal birds, though may move inland to breed. Sandpipers and plovers run about on mud, sticking their bills in it to look for worms and so on. Gulls, terns and skuas often prefer to feed at sea.

Cormorants and their relatives: A large and diverse group of mostly big, mostly aquatic birds. This group includes the cormorants (sleek, usually black, swimming and diving fish-eaters), the herons (long-legged fish-stalkers), the gannets (graceful fliers and plunge-divers) and the pelicans (whose beaks can hold more than their bellies can).

---

* Auks are penguin lookalikes, but they can fly. Just.

Parrots: Most parrots live in tropical countries, and many are very colourful – and very noisy. They have strong feet and legs for clambering about in tree tops, and hooked beaks that help them climb as well as enabling them to demolish sizeable fruits and nuts. Possibly the cleverest of birds.

Owls: Mostly night hunters, they are not closely related to the hawks, falcons and others of the predatory day shift. They have superb vision and hearing for detecting their prey in the dark. That big head is mostly eyeballs and ear canals rather than brain so they're not as wise as they look – they'd never outsmart a parrot.

Songbirds: The biggest group of all, this one includes many of our most familiar garden birds – thrushes, robins, sparrows, finches, starlings, warblers and crows all belong here. Most of them are small, most of them have pleasant songs and most of them would not look out of place perching on a branch or twig – the group is therefore often called 'perching birds'.

Birds of Britain

To really get to know and enjoy the different bird species that live in Britain, you'll need a field guide, as we have a couple of hundred breeding species, plus many more that visit in winter or stop off during their migration. Your garden or local park is a good place to start – here you should see sparrows, assorted tits, finches, crows, pigeons and thrushes, robins, dunnocks and wrens. If your park has a pond, you can probably add a couple of species of ducks and geese, plus mute swans, coots, moorhens and gulls to the list. Learning the common birds is key to recognizing something not so common when you see it. Learning a bit about how birds live can also help you figure out what's what, as well as explaining why birds do what they do.*

Love and marriage

Nearly all birds nest in the spring, so their chicks hatch at a time when the days are long and insects and other natural food is abundant. This gives them the best chance of successfully rearing the chicks, and the chicks a good chance of making it on their own once they become independent. But before any of that can happen you need to find a consenting adult to make babies with. As this can take a while, lots of birds begin the process of looking for a mate in late winter.

The courtship process depends very much on whether one parent (nearly always the female) will be going it alone, or whether the pair will be rearing their chicks together. In the case of the former, the females are very choosy, only mating with males that show exemplary physical fitness, while the males will take any chance they get to have sex with any female as they have no further investment in what happens afterwards. Courtship usually involves lots of competitive male posturing and generally showing off, and lots of critical scrutiny of said showing-off by the females.

In birds that rear their chicks as a team, both male and female can be quite choosy and expect future partners to demonstrate not only their fitness but also their parenting

---

* Don't let people call you a 'twitcher' though. Twitchers are obsessive rarity-chasers, ordinary bird-watchers are 'birders'.

skills in some form before making a commitment. Many courtship displays involve the male feeding the female – he needs to show he is a good provider as he's likely to do the bulk of the food-finding for the chicks, especially when they're small. Kittiwakes, which nest on sheer cliffs, court by trying to wrestle each other off the cliff edge, thus demonstrating their ability not to fall off a future nest.

Wandering eyes

A large proportion of bird species stick to one partner for the breeding season, and often even for life – far more so than mammals. However, birds are no saints when a tempting offer of extramarital sex is on the cards, and sneaky couplings with the neighbours happen very frequently in so-called monogamous songbird species. For a male this is a great idea as it means he might just father an extra chick or two but doesn't have to bother feeding them – the cuckolded regular partner of his fling will do that. For a female, having a mixed-paternity brood means more genetic diversity, which is always good news for survival.*

Obviously, being the unwitting victim of such cuckoldry is not good news, especially for males who can never be quite sure that any of the chicks they are rearing are truly their own. So males work hard to keep other males from coming near their ladies.

---

* It's surely only a matter of time before the BBC produces a bawdy comedy/documentary about bed-hopping sand martins, narrated by Barbara Windsor.

Why do birds sing?

For the same reason that fools fall in love, sort of. It's hormones. When you hear a bird sing, try to spot it – you'll notice how alert its posture is, how it seems to throb with excitement. That's because it's seething with testosterone. Male birds sing at the start of the breeding season when they have found an area they want to live and breed in (territory), and the song has two messages, depending on who hears it. To another male bird, it means: 'This area is my territory – don't come near it or we'll have to have a big fight.' More importantly, to a female bird it means: 'This area is my territory. Isn't it great? Aren't I a fantastic male to have found such a great territory? Want to join me in it?'

Once he has attracted a mate, the male still needs to keep singing, to defend his territory and now his mate as well. So birds sing most at the start of the breeding season, but carry on all through the summer. The 'dawn chorus' of particularly intense birdsong that wakes you up at 4 a.m. happens because sound carries particularly well at this time of day.

Some birds have lovely, inventive, moving and melodic songs. Others sound like chainsaws, farts, or someone choking to death. What can we conclude from this? Not much, except that female birds' tastes aren't always the same as ours. Woodpeckers 'sing' by whacking their bills very fast against a nice resonant bit of wood, while snipes do it by making a kazoo-like buzzing sound with their tail feathers as they fly. It all has the same purpose. Many birds throw in a dance routine with the song as well, or drop the song altogether and just do the dance – you've probably seen male ducks and pigeons bowing and posturing at the females. The vigour of

WHO SAID THAT?

Trying to identify individual songbirds from the noisy confusion of a dawn chorus is difficult but gets easier with each song you learn. There are great birdsong CDs you can buy which will help, though there's no substitute for arduously tracking down each unfamiliar singing bird you hear – this often frustrating process will help ensure you remember each one, especially if it takes ages. Here are a few pointers on identifying some common British birdsongs.

Thrushes have rich, warbling, melodious songs. Song thrushes repeat each phrase twice or more. Mistle thrushes sing loudly but without much imagination. Blackbirds have very beautiful and varied songs.

If the song is very short and very simple it's probably a **tit**. Great tits repeat two notes again and again – so do coal tits but at a higher pitch. Bluetits have a brief, rapid chatter.

Most **finches** have rather unexciting high-pitched twittering songs. The chaffinch's descends the scale and ends with a breathless flourish. The greenfinch's song includes strange nasal sneering notes. The goldfinch's could be likened to tinkling laughter, if you're in a poetic frame of mind.

In summer, **warblers** arrive from their African winter homes and add a new confusing element to the songscape. Most warbler songs are pleasant and some are quite lovely. The willow warbler's sweetly and slowly descends the scale.

The chiffchaff repeats two notes – together they sound like 'chiffchaff' – slowly. Blackcaps warble rapidly and sweetly, while reed and sedge warblers give a chuntering, ceaseless string of squeaky, rattly notes.

Of the others, **robins** sing their sweet, high-pitched and rather melancholic song all year round (most other birds go quiet in winter). They also sing at night, especially in cities.*
The song usually begins with long, drawn-out, plaintive notes, which phase into more rapid warbling. **Wrens** have a loud song for their size, with rapid machine-gun rattles in between more pleasant trilling. **Dunnocks** have a nice enough but rather nondescript warble. The simple twitter of **goldcrests** is so high-pitched that if you've trashed your ears at loud concerts in your youth you may not be able to hear it.

the song and dance tells the female how fit and macho the male is – a strong male will father strong chicks.

Nest-eggs

All birds lay eggs. Flying around with a litter of wriggling babies inside you would be hard work at best – egg-laying is basically a way of saving weight. The downside is that once

---

* Yes, it probably was a robin that sang in Berkeley Square that time. Nightingales don't like cities.

Look – I can fly 100 metres straight upwards and sing nonstop at the same time. How could a female skylark not be impressed?

laid all eggs need to be constantly kept warm (**incubated**) by the parent bird sitting on them to allow the chick inside to develop.

Because they need to be able to fly at the drop of a hat no matter what, birds lay relatively small eggs, which are formed one at a time, and most of an embryo's development takes place after the egg is laid. For an illustration of what extremes of egg size are possible if you do take flight out of the equation, look up x-ray pictures of kiwis about to lay their eggs – it's enough to make your eyes water.

So, the mother bird retains her ability to fly, but the trade-off is that the eggs have to be kept warm – body-heat warm – for the days and weeks that follow to allow the embryos inside to develop. They must be carefully sat upon (a careless claw could puncture the egg shell, and then the contents would dry out, killing the embryo), turned over from time to time and not left uncovered. Small songbirds incubate their eggs for about two weeks; for larger birds it can be much longer. The need for incubation creates a need for a nest, where both eggs (and, in due course, chicks) and parent bird will be safe during the long sit.

At home with the birds

The classic bird's nest is a cup of twigs, hidden in a tree or bush, held together with mud and lined with soft stuff like feathers or moss. Most songbirds make a nest along these lines. You've probably seen old ones in hedgerows, exposed to view when the leaves fall in autumn. Some of our little birds go for the safer – and less work-intensive – option of building inside a cavity in a tree. No need to anchor the nest to anything, just stuff the hollow with suitable material and once in you're much safer from predators. The problem is that cavities like this aren't that common in nature. Most are old, abandoned woodpecker nest holes, but with tits, nuthatches, redstarts and pied flycatchers all fighting it out for each hole, they must envy the woodpeckers, who are able to make their own. By putting up nest boxes, we provide a perfect alternative to a natural tree cavity.

Water birds tend to construct big piles of reeds and sticks at the water's edge. Placing the nest on or by a lake island rather than on the shore is a much safer option, as predatory mammals like weasels and stoats aren't keen swimmers. In many types of ducks, the female does all the nest-building and incubation alone and she often hides her nest quite well. With

FAUNA

mute swans, which form long-term pair bonds, the nest is usually in plain view, the female reclining on it fast asleep while the male restlessly patrols the lake, occasionally attacking other water birds in a fit of paranoia.

Life on the edge
Birds that nest on cliff ledges – guillemots and peregrine falcons for example – tend to take less trouble when it comes to nest-building. If the crevice is secure enough, there's often hardly any nest to speak of. Ground-nesting birds like skylarks and pheasants tend not to bother with elaborate nests either – finding a really good hiding place is paramount and there's no point drawing attention to the chosen spot by adding lavish furnishings. Ringed plovers nest discreetly on beaches and rely on their camouflage and that of their eggs to avoid predation. Terns nest on beaches too, but they form dense, noisy and highly visible colonies in which everyone is looking out for everyone else and any passing potential predators (that includes you, so be careful) get seen off in no uncertain terms by a squadron of irate, screeching, dive-bombing parents.

Sibling rivalry

Most birds lay an egg in the nest each morning until the clutch is complete, but don't start to incubate until the clutch is complete or almost complete. The embryos don't start to develop until incubation starts, so this way the whole clutch hatches at about the same time. Logistically, it's easier for the parents that way. In some species, especially owls and birds of prey, incubation begins straight away and the chicks hatch at different times. The older chicks get preferential treatment (probably because they shout the loudest and can easily boot their small siblings out of the way in the scrum for food) and in the event of food shortages they're the ones most likely to survive. In such circumstances, the big ones help nature along by attacking and beating up the little ones.*

Once the **nestling** inside the egg has grown to almost completely occupy the space available to it and is bent double in a most uncomfy position, it begins to struggle and thrash and beat away at the inside of the shell. Nestlings have a hard bit at the tip of their otherwise rather soft and floppy bills called an **egg tooth**, and this is what initially breaks the shell. Flexing movements of the little chick's body help prise the cracked shell open. The egg tooth gradually disappears as the bill firms up over the first few days after hatching.

Childcare schemes

Newly hatched baby birds come in two forms. They are either naked, blind, helpless and a little bit repulsive, or fluffy, wide-eyed, able to rush about and incredibly cute. The former are called **altricial**, the latter **precocial**. Think 'precocious' if you want to remember which is which. There's a little bit of crossover – baby birds of prey are fluffy but helpless, baby coots can move around but are breathtakingly ugly.** The key point, though, is that either the babies can leave the nest and go off into the world almost immediately, or they have to remain nest bound for some weeks, until they can walk and fly.

---

* You really don't want to be the younger of two eagle siblings.
** In a cute kind of way. 'Cugly', perhaps.

CHEATING THE SYSTEM

Parenthood is a massive stress for adult birds, so it's not surprising that a few species have done away with it altogether, opting instead to trick other birds into doing the work for them. The most notorious of these so-called 'brood parasites' is the cuckoo, a long-tailed, hawkish, migratory bird whose famous disyllabic song ushers in the spring across Western Europe.

The cuckoo's tactic is thus. Every female cuckoo specializes in a single 'host species'. In Britain, for example, most favour reed warblers, dunnocks or meadow pipits. The female cuckoo finds all the nests of her preferred host within

Problem child: a young cuckoo soon grows bigger than its reed warbler foster parents, thanks to its awesome pester power

her territory and watches them carefully. Once she has mated with a male cuckoo, she loiters discreetly around each nest in turn; when the incubating warbler, dunnock or pipit leaves the nest for a break, she sneaks in, takes out one host egg and lays her own in its place. Her eggs look very like the host's in size, colour and pattern, and the rightful owners of the nest rarely notice anything's amiss.

The cuckoo embryo develops at a furious pace, hatching before or not long after the remaining host eggs. The hatchling then sets about eliminating the competition, manoeuvring each egg or chick onto its back and then hoicking it out of the nest. Before long, the cuckoo is alone and will enjoy the undivided attention of its host parents. Although most small birds will immediately recognize and angrily attack an adult cuckoo if they see one, for some reason they don't recognize its offspring – even when the young cuckoo has grown so big that it sits on the nest like a bowling ball on an egg cup – and continue to cram food down that hungry gullet until the cuckoo baby is ready to follow its (real) parents on migration to Africa.

Birds who have precocial chicks have a much easier time as the little ones can feed themselves. Taking care of the chicks in these species, therefore, often only requires one parent. Look at the duck families on your local pond – there's Mum with nine ducklings in tow, but no Dad in sight. The male ducks, tired out from a long spring of fighting and mating, get the summer off.

For parents of altricial chicks, several weeks of hard work follow, fetching food for the youngsters from dawn until dusk. This is a two-bird job, and is the reason why birds that have altricial chicks tend to form lasting pair bonds. Often one parent stays with the chicks while the other forages when the little ones are small and still naked, but once the kids have grown some baby feathers and can keep themselves warm, Mum and Dad both have to busy themselves finding food to stuff down the chicks' capacious gullets.

Keeping it in the family: moorhens are unusual in that youngsters from earlier broods help their parents care for the next set of babies

COUNTING THE CATERPILLARS

If you have bluetits nesting in your garden, you could while away an hour observing how many times the parents visit the nest and how many caterpillars they bring in over that time. Each baby bluetit needs about 100 caterpillars a day, and each bluetit brood can be ten-strong. So the parents have to find 1,000 caterpillars a day to keep their chicks alive – it's no mean feat.

What if they don't manage it? The weaker chicks will die. In Britain's very wet summer of 2007, for example, nearly half of the country's baby bluetits starved in their nests because there just weren't enough caterpillars about.

With fewer young bluetits and other songbirds about, nesting sparrowhawks will struggle too. These predators time their nesting to coincide with small songbirds leaving their nests, as they need to bring up to ten small songbirds a day back to their nests to feed their chicks. If they can't find enough then their chicks will starve.

That's how the economics of the ecosystem work. Caterpillars control bluetit numbers, and bluetit numbers control sparrowhawk numbers. So if you see sparrowhawks hunting the little birds in your garden, don't be too downhearted about it – the presence of top predators is a good sign that everything else further down the food chain is doing well.

Flying the coop

Young birds achieve their independence gradually. Once their wing feathers have grown they will be able to fly, and with this new mobility they quickly learn to feed themselves (of course the precocial babies have already been doing this for weeks). With these skills in place, the youngsters can cut the apron strings and move away. Often in the case of songbirds, the parents have already begun a second brood and so have little

Geronimo! A young guillemot, too small to fly, leaps from its cliffside nest into the sea. Luckily it's not too small to swim.

time to chase after the first batch of babies anyway. Songbirds go through an extremely vulnerable period just after leaving the nest – **fledging** – when they can't fly very well and are still begging for food from their parents, and many are killed by predators at this time. That's why bluetits have ten or more chicks at a time – sadly most of those won't make it to adulthood.

Young birds' first feathers are often very dull-coloured. This is a good idea for two reasons – for camouflage and to keep them safe from their own parents. As soon as a spotty brown robin chick starts to sprout its first red breast feathers, the alarm bells go off in Dad's mind and the 'Another robin! Kill him!' instinct is triggered. By this point the young robin is well able to fend for itself... just as well as it will be chased away, and beaten up too if it doesn't flee fast enough.

Staying alive

At the end of the breeding season, each bird's goal is to survive until the next breeding season. Insects, summer food for so many species, become fiendishly hard to find, daylight foraging hours shorten and the nights grow cold. Birds that don't hibernate have to find other ways of getting through the cold and lean months. This often means a change of regime, sometimes quite a radical one. Here are some survival strategies you'll see in the avian world as winter approaches:

1. **Get the hell out**: Migration is one solution – just fly south and enjoy another spring and summer on a different continent. Sounds perfect, although it does entail

preparing for and surviving a long and hazardous journey. Small, insect-eating birds such as swallows, warblers and flycatchers migrate, as insects become hard to find in winter.

2. **Go to the seaside**: Temperatures stay a bit higher on the coast, so many birds that nest inland, especially in the uplands, head for their nearest shoreline in winter. They include small birds such as meadow pipits, skylarks and twites, and also such birds of prey as merlins and hen harriers.

3. **Team up**: You might be fiercely territorial in the breeding season, but in winter that's just a waste of energy. Much better to form flocks and have many eyes looking for food and checking for danger. Finches, crows and starlings form large winter flocks.

4. **Go veggie**: With insects hard to find, if you aren't going to migrate then it makes sense to switch to a plant-based diet of seeds, fruits and nuts. This is what enables insect-eaters such as robins and thrushes to survive.

5. **Make a stash**: The glut of autumn fruits and nuts is over all too soon. Some birds, including jays and coal tits, hide or bury spare food, creating a winter larder.

A few committed insect-eating birds do spend their winters in the cold. They tend to be specialized feeders, such as tree creepers, which use their long, delicate bills to search cracks in tree bark for little creatures. As several kinds of insect will spend their winters hiding in such places anyway, the tree creeper doesn't really need to change anything.

Goldcrests mostly pick their insect prey from in between pine needles, and that too remains a good foraging ground in winter.

The bird year

When you're out and about looking for birds in any country that enjoys a regular seasonal pattern, what you'll see depends very much on the time of year. Here's a quick summary:

Spring: Birds are singing, courting, mating and nest-building. Male birds are often looking at their very best to impress the females. Migratory species like swallows, swifts and many kinds of warblers arrive through spring and begin a high-speed version of the courtship process. Many of the water birds that are around in winter migrate north to the Arctic to breed.

Summer: A busy time but birds often go about the business of chick-rearing quite discreetly so you may see fewer birds than in spring. Fledglings appear through summer, and adult birds start to look a bit haggard and threadbare as the hard work takes its toll. Male ducks moult into a dull plumage (**'eclipse' plumage**) for a few weeks while growing their new flight feathers. Wetlands can be very quiet.

Autumn: The migratory birds are eating themselves silly, laying down fat stores to last them through their journey to Africa. Swallows flock over lakes to hoover up the last flying insects of the year, warblers sit in hedgerows downing berry after berry. Ducks and wading birds start to form flocks. Migrants depart through September to November – this is the peak time for rarities to be found as some migrants get lost en route and show up in unexpected places.

Winter: Woodlands and open countryside may seem very quiet, but wetlands and the coast become busy with large flocks of gulls, wading birds, wildfowl and songbirds. Inland lakes may freeze up, forcing more water birds to the coast. Winter visitors like redwings and fieldfares arrive, as do many of the ducks, geese and waders that spent their summer breeding up in the Arctic.

Fact or fiction?

Rumours abound about what wild birds do and don't do. Here a few myths and urban legends are scrutinized:

Can a swan really break a man's arm? Maybe. A territorial male mute swan will certainly attack intruding humans with furious force, and a blow from one of his wings could theoretically snap an ulna, though proven cases seem to be nonexistent.

Are those green things in London really parrots? Yes. London has a large population of ring-necked parakeets, descended from escaped pets (but probably not from the pair released in Carnaby Street by Jimi Hendrix in the 1960s).

Can birds smell it when a human has touched their nest? No, most birds have virtually no sense of smell. Don't let that be an excuse to go near birds' nests though. If they see you do it they may abandon the nest, and you could lead predators to the nest as well.

Do cats/magpies/sparrowhawks endanger songbirds? Magpies and sparrowhawks – no, they will only thrive if their prey species is doing well. Cats – maybe, as their numbers are unaffected by how many birds they kill. Domestic cats always see to it that they're fed no matter what. If you share your home with a furry killer, put a bell on its collar and keep it in overnight to give the birds a fighting chance.

Reptiles and amphibians

BRITAIN DOESN'T HAVE many wild snakes, lizards, frogs, toads or newts, and is completely lacking in tortoises, crocodiles, caecilians and salamanders. Reptiles and amphibians lack the ability to regulate their own body temperatures and rely on heat in the air around them to keep them warm enough to be active, so both groups have a hard time surviving anywhere too chilly. Those that do live in colder regions are all hibernators, spending their winters in a well-hidden and profoundly unconscious state.

The difference between reptiles and amphibians is, on the face of it, a preference for land-based living in the former and a watery world for the latter. But then crocodiles like the water, and toads spend plenty of time nowhere near it. The real differences are subtler. Reptiles have firm scaly skin, while that of amphibians is soft and non-scaly. Reptiles lay their eggs on dry land, and the eggs have tough leathery shells, but amphibians produce jelly-like spawn and always deposit this in water. Newly hatched reptiles look like 'mini-me's of their parents, but newborn amphibians are wiggly tadpoles, with many changes to undergo before they look like Mum and Dad.

Reptile roll call

Three snakes and three lizards are all Britain has in the way of native reptiles. The snakes are the **grass snake** (the biggest, lives near water and likes swimming), the **smooth snake** (the rarest, lives on heath land and likes doing as little as possible) and the **adder** (the commonest, the only venomous one, and also the one with the most striking pattern). Lizard-wise we have the **common lizard** (the, er, common one), the **sand lizard** (the rare, colourful one) and the **slowworm** (the one with no legs).

In addition to these, we now have quite a few non-native reptiles roaming our lands, largely thanks to people releasing pets that they didn't want any more and those pets proving they were just as happy in the wild. Red-necked terrapins haunt many a parkland pond, big, stripy, pointy-faced, freshwater turtles that eat unknown quantities of baby water

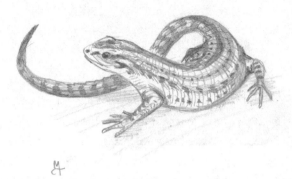

Scale model: you're more likely to see a common lizard than any other reptile, and they are exquisite little animals

birds.* On the Channel Islands live two large and impressive lizards, the **wall lizard** and the **green lizard**, and both of these have been introduced to the south coast of mainland England. Finally we have an alien snake, the **Aesculapian snake** which has a colony along the Regent's Canal in London and another around Colwyn Bay in north Wales, but it's only the terrapin that you're really likely to meet in the wild.

Snakes and adders

Seeing reptiles requires a warm day, good news for you. The first really warm day in spring is often a good time to go reptile-hunting, as this may be the first time they get active after hibernation and they'll be particularly eager to find something to eat and perhaps get busy with a mate. Heathy places with

---

* *Teenage Mutant Ninja Turtles* has a lot to answer for.

SO WHICH IS IT, THEN?

With so few species to choose from, identifying a wild reptile isn't difficult as long as you get a good look. If it has legs, it's either a common lizard or a sand lizard. The former are small, dingy grey-greenish with subtle patterning, and are very common. The latter are bigger (up to 18cm long compared to no more than 15cm for the common), stockier and more craggy-looking, a bit more dragon-like, if that helps. And the males are bright, bright green in summer.

No legs means it's a snake or a slowworm. Slowworms are small and uniformly cylindrical, lacking a distinct head and having a rather blunt tail. Look for the end with the sparkly little eyes to figure out which way round it is. They are glossy and quite uniformly greyish (or greenish or brownish). All our snakes have distinct heads and tapering tails. Adders usually have a clear black zigzag pattern running down their backs. Grass snakes are greenish with a striking yellow, black-edged collar. Smooth snakes are the most boring-looking, dull greyish with a faint pattern of darker marks.

plenty of sunny spots are ideal hunting grounds – try the New Forest or the heath lands of west Surrey, southern Dorset or the Suffolk coast.

If you're out looking for reptiles, it's particularly important to tread softly. With its whole body in contact with the ground, a snake picks up the vibrations of human footsteps quickly and easily. You might feel silly doing it, but creeping along like Wile E. Coyote in full stalk mode will improve your chances of getting close to a sunbathing reptile. If it feels you coming, it will slither or scuttle off into the undergrowth at high speed. So creep, and stop often to scan any sunny spots ahead.

Hide and seek

Reptiles also like to hide under stuff. On many a nature reserve you'll notice big sheets of corrugated metal lying around cluttering the place up, but these have usually been placed there on purpose to provide a hiding place or even a hibernating place for reptiles – they get nice and warm in the sun which makes them even more attractive to these heat-loving animals. You really shouldn't lift them up and look underneath, as you'll disturb anything hiding there, which could include small mammals and insects as well as the odd slowworm or snake. But there's nothing to stop you putting a bit of metal down in your own garden and seeing if anything moves in beneath. If you do look under the sheet, do so carefully and don't drop it back, replace it just where it was. If you don't think you can trust yourself not to drop the sheet if confronted with an angry adder beneath, best leave it alone.*

If you have a decent compost heap in your garden, it may already be home to some slowworms, which enjoy the warmth and wealth of little critters that such places have to offer. You might even get the odd grass snake laying eggs in your compost heap if you live close to good grass-snake habitat.

---

* An adder bite probably won't kill an adult. Probably best not to chance it, though.

Lizard lives, snake strategies

All of our reptiles are hunters. The lizards capture insects and other little invertebrates, while the snakes take bigger prey – small mammals, frogs and the like. Once sufficiently warmed up all the reptiles can put on an impressive turn of speed, and catch their prey with a rapid pounce. The adder's venom helps it immobilize its victim quickly, while grass snakes gulp down their prey (nearly always frogs or toads) quickly.

When they first wake up from the long winter sleep, the reptiles are keen to get mating. Typically the males find the females by their smell, and some form of courtship takes place. Adders perform an elaborate and graceful dance, while common lizards have what looks like a mutual biting contest. Once the mating season is over, the reptiles go their separate ways and live more or less alone (though in loose colonies in the case of the lizards).

The grass snake and the sand lizard lay and bury their eggs in warm places – often in piles of rotting vegetation for grass snakes, and just under the surface of the sand for the sand lizard. No further care is necessary, natural warmth does the job. The eggs are quite unlike bird eggs, having pliable leathery shells rather than brittle ones. The young develop inside over a few weeks, then hatch out as perfect mini grass snakes and sand lizards respectively. In the other four reptiles, young are born fully formed, sometimes encased in a fragile membrane but sometimes not, and are fully capable of hunting for themselves straight away.

A change of clothes

As reptiles grow they have to shed their skin, a tedious and risky business. As the time to shed the skin approaches, the old skin loosens away from the body and the reptile becomes pretty inactive. Not only does it lose its swiftness, but its vision suffers too, as the scale that protects the eye loosens away too. A few days later and it breaks free, losing the whole old skin in one piece. As shedding takes several days to complete and happens about once a month, it's a major part of snake life, but these animals have slow metabolisms and don't need to eat very often. In lizards, the skin peels off in bits and pieces, giving the poor animal the look of an under-cautious British sunbather on their first Caribbean holiday.

All change: an adder in a shiny new set of scales leaves its rumpled old coat behind

CHAMELEON KARMA

The colour-changing technology used by these tropical, tree-climbing lizards is too interesting to completely overlook. How do they do it? Their skins contain layers of specialized cells. The top layers have yellow and red pigment, the lower layers contain a substance which reflects blue light. A bottom layer contains the dark pigment melanin. The distribution of the pigment grains changes the overall colour of the chameleon, and hormone levels (influenced by what the chameleon sees and feels) can bring about these changes very rapidly, enabling it to match its surroundings.

Frogs and friends

Britain has six native amphibians, the same number as there are reptiles, which is easy to remember (though, just to ruin things, there is a seventh which may be a native too, or possibly introduced – the jury is still out). Those six comprise the **common frog**, two kinds of toads (**common** and **natterjack**) and a trio of newts (**great crested**, **smooth** and **palmate**). As with reptiles, there are several introduced species as well. All of these creatures spend the early parts of their lives in water, swimming about in tadpole form while their legs gradually grow, but all head for dry land to a greater or lesser extent once they're adult.

Like reptiles, amphibians are predators, capturing their invertebrate prey on land and in the water. Frogs and toads can fire out their sticky tongues at passing flies and other prey.

Big toads have particularly catholic tastes, eating small mammals, nestling birds and even baby grass snakes – there's revenge for you.

Frogs and toads

The common frog is our familiar, bog-standard frog with smooth, froggy skin, usually a distinctive dark bandit mask and a bouncy demeanour. The common toad is a slower, more bumbling creature, with a blunter nose, a pair of bulbous glands behind its eyes, warty skin and more inclined to stand up tall and hiss at you when threatened than to make a leap for it. Its second line of defence is the nasty-tasting stuff secreted by those warts, which convinces many a would-be predator (though not grass snakes) to drop it pronto. The rare natterjack toad is a smaller, louder version of the common, with a characteristic yellow line down its back. The common toad and common frog may show up practically anywhere, with the toad in particular sometimes found some distance from water. The natterjack lives only in a few heathy or sandy areas, mostly near or on the coast.

Newts

Newts, unlike frogs and toads, possess long whippy tails and short legs, being built for swimming rather than jumping, and spend a lot of their adult life in water, though they do come out to hibernate and live mostly on land for about a month before hibernation takes place. Courting males develop exotic frilly crests along their backs and tails, and colourful spotty patterns on their bellies. The great crested is easily the largest, a magnificent beast with warts, blackish skin and in the breeding male a dramatic jagged back crest and a distinct

HUG ME

Have you ever noticed those strange triangular warning road signs with a picture of a toad on them? It's only in early spring that they really have anything to warn you about, because this is when female frogs and toads make their way back to the ponds they were born in, to spawn. Along the way, they are intercepted by calling males, sometimes several males, which cling to the backs of the bigger females in a passionately tight embrace. Particularly sexy females might draw so many admirers that they can barely move for the weight of heaving male bodies.

Once the couples make it to the water, the spawning can take place. Despite all the apparent passion this isn't sex as we know it, as fertilization takes place outside the female's body. She releases her eggs, and he releases his sperm on top of them. The fertilized eggs quickly develop a protective coating of clear jelly, becoming the familiar dark-centred blobs.

With newts things work a little differently, the male first entrancing the female with a swishy display of swimming that show off his crest and spotty belly to their best advantage. Then he releases a package of sperm which the female deftly collects with her **cloaca** (the multifunctional orifice below her tail). Her eggs are fertilized inside her, and she then lays her eggs one at a time.

break between the end of that and the start of the smoother-edged tail crest. Of the other two, the palmate is smaller but the two are quite similar. The best way to tell them apart is to look at the throat, which is spotty in smooths, plain in palmates.

Tourists

As for the non-natives, there are **marsh frogs**, which are big, very noisy and common in the south, and the very similar **edible** and **pool frogs**.* The latter is the one that may or may not be a genuine British native – the prevailing view at the moment is that it is, though some of its populations at least are definitely introduced. Then we have the **midwife toad**, the **alpine newt**, the **bullfrog**, the **African clawed toad** and the **European tree frog**. All of these could be bad news for native amphibians because of competition for habitat and the dangers of interbreeding – and in fact the massive and voraciously destructive bullfrog is a threat to much of our wetland wildlife.

Metamorphosis

Many of us will have collected frogspawn in the hope of watching tadpoles grow up. All amphibians produce spawn: fertilized eggs that hatch out as tadpoles. With frogs the spawn comes in a big blobby cloud, with toads it forms strings. Each tadpole begins life as a big bulbous head with a tail and a pair of feathery gills, and gets around by thrashing that tail about.

---

* The edible frog is the one whose legs are a tasty treat for our neighbours across the Channel.

Becoming a frog: the amphibian life cycle

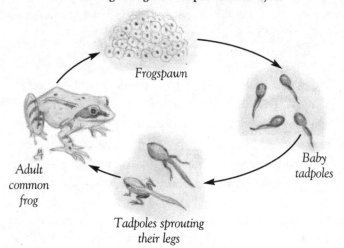

Frogspawn

Baby tadpoles

Adult common frog

Tadpoles sprouting their legs

Tadpoles are vegetarian, eating algae and fragments of water plants, but as they get bigger they start to eat small water animals. Over the next few weeks their legs grow and (in frogs and toads) those long tails gradually shrink away to nothing.

The big sleep

Amphibians, like reptiles, need to hibernate as our winters aren't warm enough for them. Their soft, water-permeable skins have to stay damp, so they pick fairly soggy sheltered spots to spend the winter. If your garden pond attracts amphibians, you'd be doing them a big favour if you provide some nice hiding places that will remain undisturbed through winter. They'll use them as hiding places in summer, too – a small, loose pile of damp decaying logs would be a good start.

WHO'S THE DADDY?

Tadpoles can be hard to identify but there are ways. **'Toadpoles'** are blacker with shorter tails than frog tadpoles — the latter also develop a golden sheen as they mature. **'Newtpoles'** have the longest tails and look more like tiny baby fish than conventional tadpoles. Also, frog and toad tadpoles grow their hind legs first and then their front legs — with newts it's the other way round.

If you'd prefer something more aesthetically pleasing and don't mind spending a few quid, you can buy special ceramic 'toad houses' which have 'wet rooms' and 'dry rooms', providing year-round comfort.

Danger signs

Amphibians around the world are having their worst time in recent history, with many species falling prey to mystery fungal infections and several now threatened by extinction. The latest research suggests the fungus is spreading fast because of global warming. If you're seeing signs of disease in amphibians in your garden or local area, it's worth talking to someone at the amphibian conservation group Froglife (www.froglife.org).

Fish

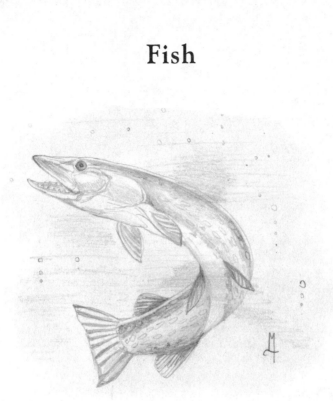

THEY'RE THE ORIGINAL vertebrate animals; mammals, birds, reptiles and amphibians all evolved from the first fish to start gulping air as they skipped about in the shallows. Today their numbers far outstrip those of the other groups, and in fact there are probably more species of fish than there are mammals, birds, reptiles and amphibians put together. But then our planet has a lot more open water than it has dry land.

Some bizarre fish

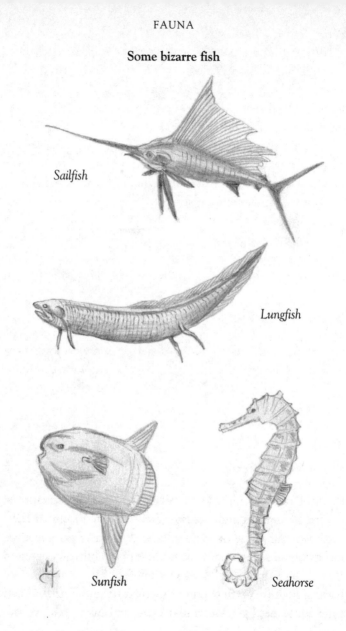

Sailfish

Lungfish

Sunfish

Seahorse

Although there are at least 30,000 species and quite probably many more, fish show a lot less variety in general shape and body plan to some other groups. The demands of living in water seem to impose certain quite severe restrictions on what's possible for fish bodies, even though invertebrate water animals come in a much more impressive variety of shapes. Or maybe fish just lack imagination. In any case, pretty much all fish have smoothly streamlined bodies, paired fins on the underside for propulsion, a tail fin for even more propulsion, and a pair of gills that enable them to extract oxygen from the water. Exceptions to this basic layout are few, but they also tend to be spectacularly odd-looking and so get a lot more attention from us than the myriad fish-shaped fish.

Some fish groups

Having established that fish classification is a big scary minefield, let's take a tentative look at some of the main groupings, with particular emphasis on those you might see in British waters:

Sharks: Yikes! Actually, don't panic. A few sharks do visit British seas but not generally the people-eating ones (and the danger of shark attacks, wherever you live, is considerably less than the risk of being killed by a herd of cows or other hostile livestock). Sharks are **cartilaginous** fish, which means their skeletons are made of cartilage rather than bone. They are mostly fast-moving carnivores, with replaceable rows of teeth.

Rays: These are cartilaginous, too, but unlike the streamlined cylindrical sharks, rays are flattened with wide 'wings' that

TAXING TAXONOMY

The classification of living things into vaguely coherent groupings is fun, especially if you're a bit geeky, but can also be wildly confusing. The four vertebrate groups we've already looked at – mammals, birds, reptiles and amphibians – each form single groups at the same taxonomic level but fish are different.

To get our heads round this, let's look at the different levels of classification, using our good selves as an example. The lowest level is the **species**, and species are grouped together in a **genus** (plural **genera**). Our species is *Homo sapiens* and our genus is *Homo* – the first word in any species' scientific name is also its genus name. We have no other species in our genus. A more populous genus is *Felis*, which contains the domestic cat, the Scottish wildcat and several other wild kitties. Next level up is **family**. Ours is Hominidae and it contains the genera *Homo*, *Pongo*, *Pan* and *Gorilla*, represented respectively by humans, orang-utans, chimps and – guess what – gorillas.*

Next level up is the **order**, and ours is the primates. Besides the apes of Hominidae, other primate families include those of the lemurs, the lorises, the gibbons and assorted monkeys. The next level up is **class**, and ours is Mammalia. Other orders in this class are Carnivora (carnivores), Rodentia (rodents) and so on. Mammalia is

---

* Scientific names aren't always Latin. There's a clam called *Abra cadabra* – disappointingly it's not magic.

one of many classes that make up the **phylum** Chordata, animals with spinal cords, which is one of several phyla to form the **kingdom** Animalia – home to every kind of animal on earth. There are numerous other classification levels in between those named here, but they are mainly super-this and sub-that – if you can remember kingdom, phylum, class, order, family, genus and species (perhaps with the handy and appropriate mnemonic 'King penguins congregate on frozen ground sometimes') you're doing fine.

Back to fish. The point about them is that, unlike the mammals, birds, reptiles and amphibians, which each comprise only one class each (Mammalia, Aves, Reptilia and Amphibia), fish comprise several classes, including the jawless fishes, the ray-finned fishes and the lobe-finned fishes. Therefore the word 'fish' is less meaningful scientifically than 'mammals' or 'reptiles', and its definition ('any non-tetrapod vertebrate that has gills all its life') is more vague. There, isn't that helpful?

they use to flap their way along. They tend to rest on the seabed, and feed there too on sea snails and the like.

Catfishes: So-called for their fleshy 'whiskers' or **barbels**, this group includes some huge species and some tiny ones, and most are bottom dwellers – spending most of their time near the bottom – in freshwater environments.

Carp: This group includes goldfish, minnows, mirror carp and many other familiar and very classically fish-shaped fish. They are mostly freshwater, snail-munching fish. The group also includes loaches and other so-called 'sucky fish' that hold their place in fast-flowing streams by sucking hard on a handy rock, and many familiar anglers' favourites such as rudd, roach and bream.

Salmon: A group of fast-swimming, strongly migratory predatory fish that live at sea and in freshwater, often both within the same lifespan. The group includes the trouts as well as salmon. They are important food fishes and are often farmed as well as being caught in the wild.

Eels: Long, smoothly tubular snake-like fish with little eyes and snapping jaws. The eel we're familiar with leads an extraordinary lifestyle involving long migrations. Other well-known species include morays and conger eels.

There are many, many more. A truly bewildering array, in fact. And seeing them is not easy, unless you're prepared to don snorkel, mask and possibly full scuba gear and enter their environment – or invest in a rod and reel and see what you can catch.

Freshwater fish in Britain

One of the things that will strike you first about many freshwater fish is how awful their names are. A lot of them sound like expletives or insults – tench, gudgeon, roach, chub. Coarse names for coarse fish. At least these fish have the sense to taste unpleasantly muddy, and so are caught just to be

SALTY OR SWEET?

Many fish can live in either fresh- or saltwater but not both. Yet quite a few can cope with different levels of salinity, so can thrive in more varied environments. Coping with water that's either more or less salty than their blood is the problem that these fish have had to solve, via the usual evolutionary pathways whereby genetic mutations produce variety and natural selection ensures the best-adapted varieties are the ones that survive and reproduce.

Sea fish lose water through their skins because of **osmosis** (the tendency of water molecules to move from low-concentrated to highly concentrated salt solutions). To get it back they must gulp seawater, but then they have lots of extra salt to get rid of. With freshwater fish, whose blood is saltier than the water they swim in, the problem is reversed – they have to get rid of excess water without losing salt from their blood. Their gills and kidneys have become adapted to do this.

To endure changes from too much salt to not enough is quite a strain for an individual fish. However, there are advantages to being able to swim in practically any water on earth. These fish can outrun parasites, can exploit the best feeding grounds at the perfect time, and can go where predators can't follow.

weighed and photographed before being released pretty much unharmed.

Several coarse fish belong to the carp family and have big grinding back teeth for eating water snails. More actively predatory freshwater fish include the fearsome pike, which eats water birds, other fish, and has no problem taking a chunk out of a careless angler should the chance arise. Another is the perch, a handsome, stripy fish that must be handled with care thanks to the venom in its fin spines.

Some common freshwater fish are too little to really interest anglers. Minnows and sticklebacks are among them. If you have a garden pond and fancy adding some fish to it, you could do worse than considering these species. Be aware that sticklebacks and amphibians don't get along, though.*

Fancy freshwater fish
The salmon and trout attract a different kind of angler – the hungry kind. These are mainly river fish in Britain, hunters of insects when they're young and predators on prawns, squids and other fish when fully grown. Fishing for these fish requires the special technique of fly-fishing, where the angler's bait is a replica fly, cast repeatedly at the river surface to imitate a real fly touching down on the surface and taking off again.

Sea fishes found off the British coast are many and varied. They include sea horses, basking sharks, sunfish and many more, including commercially important species like herring, sprat and everything you'll find battered in your local chip shop.

---

* Sticklebacks eat tadpoles. So actually from their point of view amphibians are great.

Fish tales

The fish lifecycle is, on the face of it, simple. Male and female fish get together at spawning time, the female lets loose her eggs and the male sheds sperm (in fish it's called **'milt'**) in their general vicinity. The fertilized eggs develop and hatch, and the tiny fish **fry** gradually grows to adulthood to begin the process again. Within that framework, however, there are innumerable variations in the details, and some extraordinary stories. We'll take a look at some of them.

Salmon

Our salmon swim up to cold northern rivers in the uplands to spawn in November, leaping up waterfalls in their eagerness to reach the spawning grounds. All that excitement takes its toll, for after spawning many adult salmon die. Before she pops her clogs, the mother salmon ensures her eggs are safely fixed in the gravel. There they stay through winter, hatching early the next spring.

The tiny fry live off the remains of their yolk sac after they hatch, and stay hidden in the gravel until the yolk's all gone and they have to find food for themselves. The young fry hang in the water, facing into the current and eating whatever little edible morsels are swept their way. As they grow, they seek out deeper and deeper water. After two years they are ready to migrate, and set off downstream in late spring.

The young salmon spend a year or two living in the north Atlantic and eating constantly, gaining weight and becoming fighting fit for their first spawning. Then they will go back to the estuaries and swim upstream to the same spawning grounds where they were born, to begin the process again.* The cycle repeats every two years for the rest of a salmon's life, which realistically is rarely longer than six years.

Eel

The smallest and youngest eels ever seen were found in the Sargasso Sea, an area in the middle of the North Atlantic. However, even now no-one has ever seen these enigmatic fish actually spawning, so it's still conjecture that the Sargasso Sea is where they do it. The very young eels look nothing like the adults – they are leaf-shaped, don't feed, and are quite at the mercy of the sea currents. It is only when they drift close inshore that they begin to transform into eel-shaped creatures.

These young eels are almost transparent and are nicknamed 'glass eels'. At this life-stage they start heading inland, doing so with remarkable determination and tenacity to penetrate even the smallest creeks and ditches. People have observed these eels swarming over dry land and even burrowing through wet sand. Once they find suitable fresh water to settle in they remain there for some years, feeding and growing. Then one summer they set off for the ocean again.

They stop feeding at this time and rely on stored fat to sustain them on the long journey, which once again may take them overground as well as down streams and rivers. In fact, they will never feed again, for their digestive tract dissolves away. Sex really is the only thing left to live for now... and after spawning, they all drop dead.

---

* This is the time anglers like to catch them, before they're all knackered out from spawning.

Stickleback

These feisty little fish don't undertake epic migrations, but their reproductive behaviour is unlike that of any other fish. They actually indulge in some basic parental care, which is unusual in fish, and moreover it's the dads who do it.

Each male stickleback builds a small but sturdy underwater nest, using handy riverbed materials like algae and other water plants, which he sticks together using his own kidney secretions. The gooey glue has been found to have antibacterial properties. He displays (shows off) tirelessly next to his nest, flaunting off his red belly (it only acquires this colour at spawning time) and fiercely driving off any other males that come anywhere near. When an enticingly plump, egg-stuffed female happens along, he steps up the dance, performing a frantic zigzag display that will hopefully tempt her into the nest, where she will release her eggs.

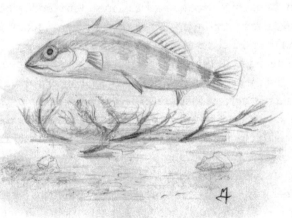

Grand designs: a male stickleback gathering waterweed to build his bachelor pad

Now the male kicks the female out of his nest, goes in and fertilizes the eggs. He spends the days up until they hatch hanging around the nest, chasing off potential predators and fanning fresh water across the eggs to make sure they get enough oxygen. Only when they hatch are his duties finished.

Fish-watching

You need a bit of imagination to watch fish. You could take up angling, and this is a great way to see lots of lake or riverside wildlife, but the fish you see will mostly be thrashing about on the end of your line rather than doing natural fishy things – a little invasive for a naturalist, perhaps.

You can see them in clear water sometimes – baby salmon and trout hanging in the current in clear, fast-flowing streams or carp sunbathing close to the surface. If you're enjoying a summer picnic on a Cornish headland, look out to sea now and then and you might be lucky enough to spot a sunfish or basking shark. Winter is a bad time for fish-watching – they tend to be much less active and stick to deeper water.

Snorkelling in British seas won't offer as technicolour a fishy experience as in the Red Sea or Great Barrier Reef, but you could see far more than you expected, particularly in the rich, clear seas off Scotland (a wetsuit might be a good idea, though). Rock pools often contain a few small marine fish, like blennies, gobies and butterfish – be patient and don't overshadow the pool if you want to see them. Finally, your garden pond may be the perfect place to watch native fish like minnows, gudgeons and sticklebacks going about their business.

Insects and other invertebrates

THINK OF AN animal, and you probably picture in your mind's eye something furry, or perhaps something scaly. That's speciesism for you, because 95 per cent of all animals are invertebrates. The author is, of course, not really helping fight this speciesism by devoting just one short chapter to this immensely diverse and overwhelmingly numerous group of animals, but hopefully this will whet your appetite to find out more about the creatures we all too often dismiss as 'creepy-crawlies' and 'weird blobby things'.

An inordinate fondness for beetles

The geneticist, evolutionary biologist and all-round super-scientist J.B.S. Haldane is responsible for that great quote 'an inordinate fondness for beetles', when asked what the biological world told us about the mind of God. One in every four animals on earth is a beetle, and beetles comprise nearly 40 per cent of the insect world. Numbers-wise, that means 360,000 species of beetles and getting on for a million described species of insects. That's just the tip of the iceberg, though, and scientists are finding new species of insects all the time. We may never catch 'em all but there could easily be upwards of 10 million insect species worldwide.

So what's it made of?

We might as well use a bog-standard adult beetle as our model for basic insect anatomy and lifestyle. It has six jointed legs, all attached to the middle body section, the **thorax**. Beetles also have four wings, the front pair modified into hard wing cases, and these are attached to the thorax as well – other insects have four normal wings, or two normal wings, or no wings at all. The head bears the two **compound eyes** (made up of lots of tiny, simple eyes), a pair of **antennae**, sensory organs that variously detect sounds, smells and temperature changes, and feeding appendages which vary greatly in form and function. The last body section, the **abdomen**, contains the gut and other important internal gubbins, and may have some clasping appendages for mating purposes but bears no wings or legs.

Beetles are among several insects that spend their early years as a very different-looking, wriggly worm-like **larva**. They form a **pupa** when mature, from which the adult insect (or **imago**) breaks out in due course. Other insects, including dragonflies, undergo a simpler transformation, the adult form breaking straight out of the skin of the immature form (in these species, the immature is much more mobile and adult-looking, and is called a **nymph** rather than a larva).

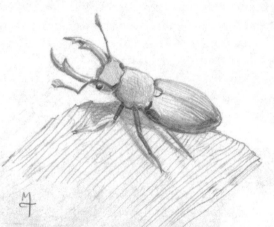

If beetles really do rule the world this might be their king –
the splendid stag beetle

Insect nation

The many insects that live in Britain fall mainly into a surprisingly manageable number of main groups, and what's more, you'll be familiar with most of them, even if you think you're not.

Beetles: We looked at them already. Wing cases and wings. Most fly, but generally spend more time travelling on foot. Often colourful. May be swift-moving carnivores, carrion-feeders or gentle vegetarians.

Butterflies and moths: The two pairs of wings are large and covered with coloured scales. Most feed on plants as larvae (caterpillars) and on nectar as adults. Butterflies are probably the most popular of insects, fighting it out with honeybees for top spot.

Winging it: a flying butterfly's four wings can all move reasonably freely, and are much more flexible than you might think

Bees, wasps and ants: Fascinating insects, many of them highly social, others practising the most gruesome forms of parasitism imaginable. All but the worker ants have two pairs of wings. They feed on all sorts of stuff, from fruit and nectar to other insects and carrion.

Dragonflies and damselflies: Long-bodied, four-winged, often colourfully metallic-looking aerial predators of other insects. Their early lives are spent as aquatic, fiercely predatory nymphs. Dragonflies are big and zoomy, damselflies small and fluttery. Both have amazingly big eyes.

Flies: The scientific name for this order is **Diptera**, which means 'two wings'. The true flies thus have just two wings. The very diverse group includes bluebottles, mosquitoes, midges, 'daddy long-legs' (crane flies) and many other vilified creatures.

Caddis flies: One of several groups of four-winged insects that live underwater in their youth. Caddis flies have long antennae and patterned wings. Other similar groups include the stoneflies, mayflies, snake flies and scorpion flies.

Bugs: It's the nickname we give to every kind of insect, all insect-like creatures and even viruses and bacteria, but 'bug' has a real meaning in biology. It's a group of vaguely beetle-like critters with sucking mouthparts. Some are winged, some wingless. The group includes cicadas, froghoppers and pond-skaters.

Grasshoppers and crickets: See, told you most of these would be familiar… These are mostly vegetarian insects, often with long, strong hind legs for bouncing away from danger. They have two pairs of wings and are noisy for insects, making chirping sounds by rubbing their wings or legs together.

All change

Insects are the poster children for metamorphosis, with many groups going through four very distinct stages of life. The minor miracle of caterpillar becoming butterfly is careworn through use as a metaphor for any kind of positive transformation.*

The first stage is the egg, laid on a suitable food plant by the female butterfly. From this little capsule emerges a tiny caterpillar, whose first action is to eat its own eggshell. It then gets to work on the plant, munching away the flesh of the leaves and growing fast, moulting its skin several times on the way. Before too long it has grown to its full size, and we can take a proper look at it. It's more like a worm than a butterfly at first glance, but there are the six legs near the front of the body, on the segments that will become the thorax. Further down the body are another few pairs of leg-like bumps, but they are not true legs. There's little sign of wings, and the head is totally different to an adult butterfly's, with chewing mandibles instead of a nectar-sucking proboscis.

The caterpillar now seeks a safe place to turn itself into a **pupa**, perhaps dangling from a plant stem like a dead leaf, or tucked into the roll of a grass blade. Its skin moults for the last time, and what's underneath becomes the pupa, a casing inside which the caterpillar body transforms into the butterfly body. The main change is the wing development, but numerous other changes go on too, all fuelled by the leaves the caterpillar consumed through its lifetime.

---

* And, in the case of *The Very Hungry Caterpillar*, the perils of overeating.

Have you had a haircut or something?

Once the butterfly is fully formed, it breaks through the **pupal shell** and clambers free, usually hanging onto the pupa for an hour or so while its crumpled little wings fill up with blood, expand, flatten and stiffen. If you're lucky enough to see this happening, you'll also notice its fat, swollen abdomen shrink and straighten, the last traces of caterpillar-hood disappearing. Then it's off into the world of flight, to find a mate and begin the process again.

Short cuts

This complete metamorphosis can be observed in wasps, bees, ants, flies and beetles as well as butterflies and moths. Other insects skip the pupa stage and go straight from nymph to adult, with the wings being the main difference between the two stages. A dragonfly nymph roams the riverbed like some nightmarish alien, spearing prey with its projectile lower jaw. When it's full-grown, it climbs up a handy water plant into the fresh air, and clings very firmly to its perch. Now, the adult dragonfly inside loosens itself from the shell of the nymph's skin and cracks its way out. Like the new adult butterfly, it has to take some time redistributing its body fluids and pumping up its wings. When it flies away, the perfect wafer-thin nymph shell remains, clinging fast to its perch with empty legs. The shell is called an **exuvium**, and you can find them attached to reed stems in spring.*

Insects are mostly inactive through winter, so all this development takes place in spring and summer. The

---

* They're great for scaring insect-phobes. Not that you should, really.

Life cycle of an orange-tip butterfly

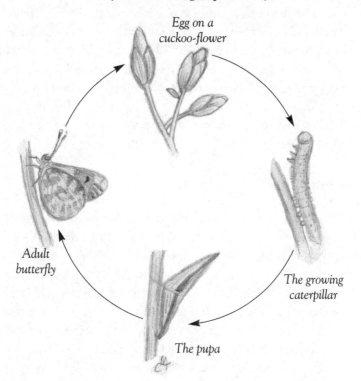

*Egg on a
cuckoo-flower*

*Adult
butterfly*

*The growing
caterpillar*

The pupa

underwater nymphs are an exception, but land-based insects mainly hibernate over winter, whether as egg, larva, pupa or adult.

Variations on a theme

Insect lifestyles run the whole gamut of possibilities. Like the so-called higher animals, they demonstrate impressive social structures, devoted parental care, elaborate courtship

Life cycle of a common blue damselfly

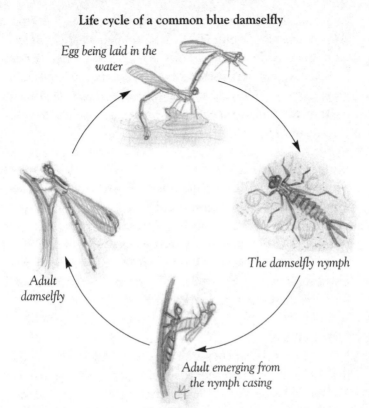

Egg being laid in the
water

The damselfly nymph

Adult
damselfly

Adult emerging from
the nymph casing

behaviour and an array of feeding strategies from the inventive to the totally macabre. We can only look at a few of the most interesting oddities here, but these are all things you could observe in your garden or on an average country walk.

Hive mind

Honeybees and ants are our best-known social insects. The large colonies are mainly staffed by the workers, which cannot reproduce. They do the construction, find the food and tend the youngsters, while one or a few queens do the breeding. Ants co-operate to bring large food items (including insects much larger than themselves) back to the nest, while honeybees tell each other about good nectar-collecting grounds through the medium of dance, wiggling in figure-of-eights which somehow convey accurate grid references to their hive-mates.*

Stuff of nightmares

Some wasps are social, but others are solitary, and some solitary wasps have the most horrible habits, laying their eggs on other living insects that then get eaten alive by the wasp larvae. Even worse than this, some solitary wasps paralyze their prey with a sting, then cart it off and stuff it in a burrow before laying eggs on it. The paralyzed insect becomes a supply of fresh but immobile food for the wasp larvae. Nasty.

Nest-builders

Not all insect babies are as tough as young dragonflies. Some make a protective home for themselves to ward off predators. Caddis fly larvae build a little portable sleeping bag around themselves out of tiny stones and other riverbed bits and pieces. Froghopper nymphs produce a blob of froth around themselves – the so-called cuckoo spit which you'll see scattering the vegetation in spring, as though a group of very impolite hikers has just gone by. In this bubbly nest the baby froghoppers can grow and feed in safety.

---

* Thus inspiring the name of the tasty honey-scented beer, 'Waggle-dance'.

Love perfume

Moths are probably the most famous producers of **pheromones** – sexy smells, if you like, in the animal world. The aroma of a female moth is so enticing that entomologists of old used them to attract lots of males for their collections. The female emperor moth, a beautiful furry heath land creature with big eye-shaped spots on her wings, produces a particularly potent whiff even while still in her pupa. When she does emerge, the first thing she'll see will be numerous eager males, and she will probably have copulated before she's taken her first flight.

Other things that scuttle

If it has more than six legs it's not an insect. It is, however, an **arthropod**, or animal with jointed legs and (usually) a tough **exoskeleton**. Besides insects, the arthropod group contains the spiders, scorpions, centipedes and millipedes, and also the **crustaceans**. Crustaceans are mainly water animals (the woodlouse is an exception) and include crabs, prawns and lobsters. And, rather bafflingly, barnacles. For some reason, we're much happier to eat them than we are to snack on insects (though this is not the case in other, more adventurous cultures).

There are more than 50,000 species of crustaceans in the world. Some live in fresh water, like crayfish and tiny critters like water fleas (**daphnia**), but your best bet for seeing them is to head for the seaside. Several species of crabs live on our shores. You're most likely to see the bigger species, like the edible crab and spider crab, in the fishmongers or lying dead in the tide-line, but pretty little porcelain crabs live in rock

ARACHNOPHOBIA

You may find them all equally horrifying, but in many parts of the world we have little to fear from spiders. They do all have a venomous bite to paralyze their prey, however, although relatively few have jaws big and strong enough to break human skin. Given the prevalence of really dangerous spiders in some parts of the world, perhaps arachnophobia is not such an irrational fear after all. The species you are most likely to encounter are:

- **Garden spider**: This is the one that spins a large, handsome web and sits proudly in the middle of it, waiting for flies to blunder in. Female garden spiders are much larger than males and are especially plump and eye-catching in autumn, when they are ready to lay their eggs. When they're like this you can clearly see the neat, white cross markings on their big, fat bodies. The big, yellow ball of eggs hatches the next spring.

- **House spider**: The big, sturdy, leggy one that lives in your shed. Its web is often a triangle spun across a corner of a room. If you're not a fan, just be glad that the related giant house spider is much rarer.

- **Daddy long-legs**: It's got a pinhead body supported (but only just) on very long and very spindly legs, which give it a wobbly but surprisingly rapid gait. The web is flimsy and hard to spot. These spiders often live indoors, too.

Leggy beauty: at least the daddy long-legs spider doesn't have a big fat hairy body to go with those absurdly attenuated appendages

- **Wolf spider**: This one doesn't spin a web, but chases its prey down on foot. It has a long, pointy-tipped body marked lengthways with subtle dark and light stripes, and long, serviceable legs – the front two pairs held characteristically close together.

- **Zebra spider**: A sweet little arachnid, this is a jumping spider with relatively short legs and a black-and-white body. It doesn't make a web but pounces on its insect prey. You'll often see it on brick walls and paths.

pools. So do the soft-bodied hermit crabs, which live inside old whelk or periwinkle shells. All have a pair of claws to grab prey and nip at predators.

Shelling out

We use the word 'shellfish' to mean both crustaceans and **molluscs**, which is as unscientific as having a catch-all term to encompass vertebrates and sea urchins. Molluscs are animals with soft bodies and hard shells. Most live in water, but there are, of course, land snails and slugs, too, with tiny or nonexistent shells. The **gastropod** molluscs (like snails) have a single shell and can usually move around quite well, albeit slowly, while **bivalve** molluscs (like mussels) have a pair of shells that they can open up or draw together, and they can hardly move at all. Gastropods tend to feed actively, while bivalves are filter-feeders, sifting out scraps of edible stuff from the water that whooshes past their open shells. Depending on moving water means they are most common in tidal areas.

The other main molluscs are the octopuses, squids and cuttlefish. Their shells are internal, and they are much more mobile than other molluscs, able to swim rapidly by taking in then shooting out jets of sea water. You'll be hard pressed to see them alive unless you do some snorkelling or diving, but you may find the chalky white shells of deceased cuttlefish on the beach (as well as in budgie cages – they provide an easy source of calcium for cage birds). You'll also find the discarded shells of other molluscs on the beach, including those of razor-shells, slipper limpets, oysters, clams, cockles and scallops.

If you're still at that rock pool, look out for molluscs like limpets, whelks, top-shells and winkles.

Worms and other squishy and spiky things

There are many different kinds of worms in the world. The ones you'll know best are the **annelid** or segmented worms, because that's the group to which garden earthworms belong. Many of the other kinds live in the sea, or are parasites of larger animals. Worms lack legs but can have quite elaborate feeding appendages. **Nematodes** or roundworms are among the most numerous animals on earth, living in and on land, fresh water, sea and inside other animals in staggering abundance. It's said that if you take away all the land but left the nematodes behind, the contours of the planet as we know them would still be recognizable.*

The jellyfish, sea urchins, starfish, sea anemones and sponges are among the other animal groups you may encounter while you're at the seaside, and they help illustrate how much richer animal life at sea is than on land, and how much less we know about it. Jellyfish and sea anemones both trap drifting prey in their stinging tentacles, but the jellyfish swim freely while the anemones are rooted to the spot like underwater flowers. Sea urchins and starfish move around the seabed (the latter more easily than the former), feeding on algae, other seabed animals and general detritus. Sponges are motionless, squashy and simple animals that feed on bacteria and other tiny scraps that the moving sea water carries past them.

---

* Welcome to Nematode-world. Population: nematodes.

Microbes

Now we're in the realm of 'things you can't see', and many of these are not actually classed as animals. Our interest in protozoans, bacteria and viruses tends to be limited to how ill they can make us if we somehow get them in our lungs, stomachs or skin. With a good microscope you can see single-celled animals like **amoebas** and **euglenas** swimming about in a drop of pond water, but these creatures don't really feature in the lives of most wildlife observers. Nevertheless, we do need to acknowledge how important they are when it comes to keeping life on earth alive.

PLANET EARTH

Ecology

WHEN YOU'RE BACK from your country walk, have a think about all the species of plants and animals you've seen – and all the species that you might have gone past without noticing, including insects, birds, maybe a few mammals, plenty of flowering plants and a selection of trees. Together, they form a web of life, eating each other, living on or in each other, competing, co-operating and generally coexisting in something approaching harmony. This is ecology – the way living species fit together to form an **ecosystem**.

Don't think of an ecosystem as an inflexible thing, absolutely dependent upon all of its parts. It's more like a living creature – it can adapt, can accommodate changes, can compensate for losses and take new opportunities. But damage too much of it all at once and it will die. That's what we're in danger of doing to many of the ecosystems in our world – breaking them too quickly and too thoroughly for any recovery to be possible.

PYRAMID SCHEMES

In terms of numbers, nature works like a pyramid. The bottom layer comprises those living things that can get their nutrients and make their energy from non-living stuff – that's basically plant-life. If the layer of plant-life is big enough, there's room for another layer on top, of animals that eat plants. But by necessity they can never become so numerous that they eat all the plants. If plants ever become locally rare, the plant-eaters' numbers will fall because some individuals won't find enough to eat. With enough plant-eating animals, there's room for another layer of the pyramid – predators. Just as with the plant-eaters, their numbers are controlled by the availability of food supplies. There will always be more finches than sparrowhawks, and more caterpillars than bluetits, because a decline in prey will trigger a decline in predators – the system is self-regulating.

Lots of goldfinches eat thousands of teasel seeds. A few sparrowhawks eat some of the goldfinches. Ecology in action.

This is a major simplification, of course, but hopefully gets the point across. We do like to say that all animals are equal, but really from an ecological point of view the ones at the top of the pyramid are less important than those below. If you take out one whole layer, all the layers above it are going to collapse.

Ecosystems near you

You need look no further than your own garden, if you have one (a typical town park is a good substitute if you don't). Take a close look and you'll see many inter-relationships between the different living things there. The plants there are mainly independent entities, living off the soil and sun. A few plants depend on other plants though. Ivy is one, it climbs up trees (and walls, and anything else that keeps still long enough) to get a share of tree-top light without going to the trouble of building a tree trunk over many years. Ivy doesn't pinch its host plant's nutrients, though; it just uses it for a leg-up.

Mistletoe, another plant that lives up trees, is a true parasite, stealing nutrients from its host tree. It doesn't climb its way up either, but relies on birds like the mistle thrush to spread its seeds through tree tops. Mistletoe fruits are tasty to these birds, and the sticky seeds get wiped on the branches when the thrush excretes them.*

Native plants support many plant-eating animals, such as caterpillars, sap-sucking bugs, flower beetles, mice, squirrels, deer and so on. Many plants need insects to pollinate them, so offer nectar within the flowers as an incentive. However, no plant wants its foliage eaten, so plants have evolved many measures to discourage them, such as ragworts' toxins in the cells, nettles' stinging hairs, thistles' spikes and London plane's bark that falls off in flakes. The plant-eaters in turn evolve counter-measures to overcome these. It's a timeless dance that you can see going on in the natural world all around you – plants trying not to be eaten by insects, insects trying not to be eaten by birds, birds trying not to be eaten by other birds and so on.

---

* If the mistle thrush ever invents toilet paper, the mistletoe will be in trouble.

Going undercover

Many insects possess what's commonly called 'warning colouration'. This is easy to spot, because the insect wearing it is, well, easy to spot. Instead of camouflage, it has bright, striking colours that no predator would miss, and indeed many of them will attract a predator's attention and be attacked. But the attack will prove costly for the predator – a wasp will sting, a garden tiger moth will taste revolting and have to be spat out – and so a valuable lesson is learnt. The next time the predator encounters a wasp or a garden tiger moth, it will recall what happened before and give the colourful creature a wide berth.

One of the most fascinating prey tricks is called **Batesian mimicry**. Here we have an animal that is perfectly harmless and absolutely delicious, but looks just like something dangerous or bad-tasting. The predator who's received a painful wasp sting won't be taking any chances tackling a hover fly that looks like a wasp. Batesian mimicry is widespread, but the mimics can't overdo it. Too many tasty wasp-alikes and the aversion therapy stops working, or doesn't work quickly enough.

Introduce yourself

At various points in this book you might have noticed mention of species that are 'non-native' or 'introduced'. These are species that have historically evolved and lived in Country A, and some of them have been set loose in Country B by humans, either accidentally or on purpose. Perhaps the most famous – and disastrous – example is the introduction of rabbits to Australia. In Britain, the grey squirrel and the

Canada goose hail from North America, while other beloved species are non-natives, too, including the horse chestnut tree. On the other hand, Britain has introduced plenty of creatures to other countries in the world: foxes to New Zealand, mute swans to South Africa and house sparrows practically everywhere.

What's the big deal?

Good question. We have no problems with people travelling the world and settling in new countries, so why should it be different for animals? The difference is that all people are the same species, so we aren't going to wipe ourselves out through competing for resources, preying on each other or producing inter-species hybrids that can't breed. With animals, non-native species can do all those things, and plants can do three of them.

We've already seen how grey squirrels carry a disease that's lethal to red squirrels. An example of the 'death by sex' scenario is provided by the ruddy duck and the white-headed duck. The former is native to North America, the latter to southern Europe, but they are closely related. Ruddy ducks, escaped from ornamental wildfowl collections in Europe, enjoy a lot of success courting and mating with white-headed ducks. That means that white-headed ducks are not making more white-headed ducks but instead white-headed/ruddy hybrids, making the rare white-headed species even rarer.

A knotty problem

The Japanese knotweed is an invasive non-native plant, which is such a tough and tenacious grower that it can displace other, weedier native plants in all sorts of habitats. Another out-competitor is the ring-necked parakeet from India, which is aggressive enough to kick stock doves, nuthatches and other native birds out of their tree-hole nests. Good nest sites are a scarce resource and the usurped birds may not breed that year.*

Supply and demand

Predation is a slightly less worrying scenario, as a predator cannot wipe out its food supply and still survive. However, it can conceivably wipe out a part of its food supply, especially if that part of the food supply is totally ill-equipped to cope with it. A classic example of this is the introduction of stoats to New Zealand, in a bid to control that country's burgeoning rabbit population (also introduced). Stoats naturally prey on rabbits in Europe, so what could possibly go wrong? Plenty, as it turned out. The stoats did eat the rabbits, but they found the native birds of New Zealand much easier prey because these birds had lived for millennia in a land entirely free of predatory mammals. Their evolved lifestyles made no allowance whatsoever for the possibility of stoats, and the stoats had a complete field day.

Change and decay

Introduced animals represent the thing that an ecosystem often can't deal with – sudden and major change. Dramatically modifying habitats by building motorways through them is another example of the same thing. Ditto

---

* That's why we need to put up lots of nest boxes. Put one on your Christmas list (or, more usefully, nail it to your shed).

WHY DO WE DO IT?

The unfortunate human habit of transporting animals and plants to new lands seems like a blatantly bad idea to us today, but we have the benefit of hindsight. With no real understanding of how ecosystems worked, people would look at a newly discovered country's assemblage of species and think to themselves, 'nice, but needs more robins'. Many introductions were just that – people wanted familiar and much-liked species from home. Most of New Zealand's common songbirds are introduced British species.

Other species have been introduced for hunting purposes – deer, rabbits and assorted game birds fit this category. Then there are the many accidental introductions – species we brought over intending to keep captive which then escaped (lots of colourful cage birds, farm animals, ornamental plants), and species which we didn't mean to bring in at all but which hitched a ride on our ships or planes (rats, which have travelled the world as sneaky boat passengers, and various others, like the geranium bronze butterfly from southern Africa, which reached Britain on consignments of potted plants).

Not all introductions succeed. For decades there have been a couple of small colonies of red-necked wallabies in Britain, descended from safari park escapees, but they have never really become very numerous. The introduced Lady Amherst and golden pheasants are close to extinction in Britain, unlike the (also introduced) ring-necked or bog-standard pheasant. Not all introductions are disastrous, either. If the species' country of origin is not too far away, it may already be equipped to coexist with some or many of our native species, and they with it. The little owl was introduced to Britain but is native to mainland Europe – it has fitted into British fauna with no obvious problems at all.

pollution, global warming, land drainage and many other things we do to make the world suit our needs better. Ecosystems survive the same way species do – by evolving. In every generation, only the best-adapted individuals of each species will survive, and will pass on those good genes to their offspring. Variety is provided by the genetic mutations that make the young a little bit different to their parents. It's a beautifully simple and stable process that enables species to accommodate change – but it takes a long time. If the change is too fast, species start to disappear, and too much of that cripples the ecosystem.

That's why ecology matters, and it's not just a philosophical matter – we are involved, intimately, and our own future is at stake. The loss of the tiger from the earth would be a terrible tragedy, but the loss of the honeybee and other pollinating insects would be a total catastrophe: our crops would fail and millions would die. There's no getting away from it: we need animals and plants for more than just something to admire and go all dreamy about.

The richer an ecosystem, the more species it contains, the more resilient it is to change – the more room for manoeuvre it has. And ultimately all ecosystems are connected. Therefore, it's in our interests to look out for wildlife, in both senses of the phrase, and champion it for our own sakes. We might still have to pack up and leave the earth one day anyway – Stephen Hawking thinks so and he knows a thing or two – but we'd be hard-pressed to find another planet as wonderful as this one.

Outside influences

LIFE ON EARTH has a lot to contend with. Although our planet is basically hospitable, it's also restless, with extreme weather and geological upheaval going on all the time. This side of the natural world is fascinating and scary in equal measures – most of us enjoy watching a good storm from safe inside, but there's always that frisson of anxiety that we could be flooded out, lightning-struck or blown away. Those who like their frisson with extra chips go tornado-chasing, volcano-gazing and monster wave surfing – we might dub them lunatics but we can't argue that they have a pretty detailed insight into the real meaning of nature's power.

Weather

Our planet lives inside a capsule of gases – an **atmosphere** – that are held there by earth's gravity and shield us from the crushing vacuum of space. Our atmosphere is made of that particular mixture of gases that we like to call 'air' – it's 78 per cent nitrogen, 21 per cent oxygen and most of the remaining 1 per cent is argon, an inert gas similar to helium. Carbon dioxide forms a tiny but important fraction of a per cent of it. Nitrogen is more or less inert, meaning it doesn't readily react with other elements. We breathe it in and let it out again unchanged, unlike oxygen, which we exhale as carbon dioxide.*

Our atmosphere can be divided into several distinct layers. The one of interest right now is the **troposphere**, the bit that's closest to the earth's surface, because this is where weather happens. The outer layers are much deeper but contain much less actual gas, eventually fading out to nothing at all. The troposphere contains virtually all our atmosphere's water vapour, and is constantly taking up water vapour from the sea through evaporation in Place A while dumping it back down again as rain or snow in Place B. Water vapour is held in the

---

* The high oxygen content of the earth's atmosphere developed after plant life evolved and took over the planet – oxygen is a plant waste product (see the Trees section for more on this).

troposphere in the form of clouds, and rain falls when the vapour cools to form droplets which eventually become too big to remain floating in the air. If this process happens very rapidly, due to lots of warm air and lots of cool air moving about, the energy discharged will produce a full-on thunderstorm.*

CLOUD-WATCHING

Clouds contribute much to the beauty of our skies, especially at sunrise and sunset. A cloudless sunset is, frankly, a bit boring. Of course, clouds also cut off direct sunshine (though they are nowhere near thick enough to cut off sunlight, hence we can still see where we're going on cloudy days) and for that they're less popular.** Clouds come in several distinct types, all associated with particular weather conditions. Here are some of them, and the weather they might bring.

Cirrus: These are high, white, wispy clouds, also called mare's tails. The water in them is held as ice. A few mare's tails don't mean much weather-wise. If there are lots of them, they can form a solid sheet called **cirrostratus**, and this may mean a storm's a-brewin' – or that one has just passed (but then you probably noticed that).

---

* Or a hurricane, or a tornado. Something much worse than nice weather for ducks, anyway.
** Although they do help save us from sunburn and skin cancer.

Cirrocumulus: High, white, fluffy little clouds, often organized in rows, sometimes forming a mackerel pattern. They're made of water rather than ice, and tend to quickly develop into another cloud form or disappear.

Altostratus: Mid-level, uniform whiteish-grey clouds that produce boring, overcast days. They tend not to bring worse than light drizzle though.

Cumulus: Low, big, fluffy white clouds. They look pretty in a summer sky, but may develop into cumulonimbus clouds that are rather more sinister (in so far as a cloud can be sinister).

Cumulonimbus: Low, big, fluffy, white and grey clouds. They are grey beneath, and if you see them from far off you may also see the haze of rain falling from them. They bring heavy rain and sometimes storms.

Wind

Wind is formed when you eat baked beans. The other kind of wind is formed when dense air meets less dense air, causing the former to rush into the latter. Air density is determined by the amount of water vapour held in the air and by its temperature, and both of these are strongly influenced by what's under the air at the time – sea, land, mountains, valleys. Because these features tend to stay more or less in the same place, wind patterns and directions are quite predictable, although wind strengths can vary a lot. Winds can shift clouds around a lot as well, producing changes in rainfall.

Climate change

The earth is hot around the middle and cold at the ends. How do we find the ends and the middle of a sphere though? (Or an almost-sphere – the earth is actually a slightly squashed sphere shape, or in techno-speak an **oblate spheroid**.) The answer lies in the way the earth spins. If you picture the earth as a spinning top (a round one), the poles are at the top and the bottom. Any given point around the middle travels a long way relative to points closer to the poles.

The North-South axis around with the earth spins is tilted 23.5° from the vertical, and this is what gives us our seasons: different parts of the planet are tilted more towards or away from the sun at different times. Without the tilt, we'd have the same relative amounts of daylight everywhere throughout the year, and no seasons. As it is, for half of the year the northern hemisphere is tilted more towards the sun, creating a summer season while the southern hemisphere experiences winter; the situation is reversed for the rest of the year.

This effect is most pronounced at the poles, which get constant daylight for some of the year and constant darkness for the rest, with a pretty abrupt transition between the two; the equator, meanwhile, gets about the same hours of daylight all through the year. If you're midway between equator and poles, you'll get long days and short days with prolonged transitional periods – a summer and a winter, and a spring and autumn. The parts of the earth that experience the four distinct seasons are called the **temperate** zones.

Spinning seasons

The northern hemisphere is in midwinter as the new year begins, and our summer falls in the middle of the year. This is reversed in the southern hemisphere. On the equator there are no distinct seasons as determined by day length, but instead there is often a 'rainy' and a 'dry' season. Equatorial animals tend to do their breeding in the rainy season and do their 'let's just try to stay alive' in the dry season. In the polar summer, many animals migrate there to breed, taking advantage of the long days, but the poles are virtually deserted in winter. A notable and famous exception is the emperor penguin, the males sitting out the dark freezing months in a big, almost motionless huddle, each one living off his body fat and incubating on his feet the single egg left there by his mate before she left for a winter of living it up catching fish in the Antarctic sea.*

Hot flushes

The earth's rocky crust isn't standing still. It's just moving around very slowly, but when the slabs of crust (**tectonic plates**) come together there can be fireworks. Volcanoes form at plate junctions, or geological **fault lines**.

Our earth has a core of molten rock and iron. It's insanely hot and very pressured in there, and sometimes all that energy makes itself felt up here on the surface. Volcanoes are holes in the earth's crust that go all the way down to the earth's

---

* One day, a scientist will discover whether penguins are capable of experiencing emotional bitterness.

Smoke signals: active volcanoes may pump out increased amounts of gases (mainly sulphur dioxide) as a precursor to an eruption

mantle, and sometimes act as pressure valves, unleashing ash, molten rock (**lava**) and lots of heat from within.

Most of us are fortunate enough not to live too close to any active volcanoes, but you only need look at Pompeii to see how devastating a big eruption can be. Rumour has it that animals are sensitive to the little vibrations and other changes that precede a volcano blowing its top, and so they can leave, but that's not much use if it happens on a small island. The volcano on the island of Montserrat in the Caribbean caused major damage between 1995 and 1997, and its **endemic** (occurring nowhere else) wildlife has been devastated. The Montserrat oriole, a pretty songbird, lost two-thirds of its habitat and is now critically endangered.

Iceland is another area with lots of volcanic activity. Besides several volcanoes, the country has many geysers. These are smaller cracks in the crust, which spout jets of hot water

ROCK ON

Rocks and water don't have that much in common at first glance, but our world is basically made of rock and water. Over very long timescales, rock is subject to a cycle that changes it from one state to another: volcanic activity, erosion and plate tectonics are all involved in this apparent metamorphosis. Fortunately, rocks stay the same long enough for us to figure out what kind they are.

- **Igneous rocks** are formed from volcanic activity. The **magma** volcanoes spout is molten rock, which eventually cools and solidifies. They tend to be either coarse-grained or glassy. Rocks of this kind include granite and obsidian.

- **Sedimentary rocks** are formed by compression (usually exerted by moving water) on fragments of older rocks and other hard stuff, such as the ground-up shells of long-dead sea snails. Limestone and sandstone are examples of sedimentary rocks. They are usually fine-grained and uniform-looking.

- **Metamorphic rocks** are somewhere in between – they are either sedimentary or igneous rocks that have been much altered by heat and/or pressure. They often show features of both igneous and sedimentary rocks.

The rock cycle, in a nutshell, is as follows. Water pressure creates solid sedimentary rocks from the fragments of hard material (including the eroded remains of older rocks) that are carried in the water. The pressure pushes these rocks down into the earth as they form. As the rock is pushed deeper, heat from the earth's core further compacts the rock – this is when it goes through its metamorphic stage – and eventually melts it into magma. Released magma from volcanic eruptions cools down to form igneous rocks, which over time are worn down by wind and water erosion to form the basic material to make new sedimentary rocks.

skywards at predictable intervals. Volcanic action off Iceland produced a new island in 1968, called Surtsey, which has provided a fantastic opportunity for scientists to study how wildlife colonizes a new piece of land from day one. Many island chains have been produced by volcanic activity, so it's not really fair to regard them as completely destructive. No volcanoes, no Hawaii.

Seismic shudders

Earthquakes are caused by energy released along fault lines by moving tectonic plates, and can be utterly devastating, especially to us humans with our easily shake-down-able buildings.

An earthquake under the sea can produce massive tidal waves (**tsunamis**) and the world learned in December 2004 how much damage they can cause. This tsunami took more than 200,000 human lives, and wrecked miles and miles of coastline wildlife habitat throughout Southeast Asia. Yet for every disaster there are opportunists waiting in the wings to take advantage of a new set of environmental conditions. When the dinosaurs went, the mammals seized their chance. When a tree is blown down in a storm in your local forest, thousands of pioneering new plants are soon springing up in the space left behind. Our planet may be violent at times, but that violence has helped to make it what it is.

Earth's neighbours

THEY SAY IT'S a profound and humbling experience to look back from the moon and see the earth in its entirety, a pretty little blue disk adrift in a sea of nothing. Look outwards at the latest 'deep field' images from the Hubble telescope and you'll see more galaxies than you can count, each one billions of stars strong. Douglas Adams wasn't kidding when he described the universe as 'big' and ourselves as 'insignificant'. Yet we do exist, and we have our place in the cosmos. In this section we look at some of the other nearby heavenly bodies that we can see from here on earth.

The moon

We have just the one moon, unlike some of the other planets in our solar system, but ours has an important influence upon the earth. Our moon is a big round chunk of rock,* about 250,000 miles from earth. It orbits earth, taking about twenty-seven days to go all the way around earth and get back to where it started. However, it takes about twenty-nine-and-a-half days to move through all its phases (from new moon to full and back again) – that's because a bit extra is added due to earth's own movement around the sun.

How the moon looks to us depends where it is relative to the sun. The moon doesn't produce its own light, it just reflects that of the sun. Therefore the different moon shapes we see through the month depend how much sunlight bounces off it and reaches it, and we call them the phases of the moon.

Don't worry, it's just a phase

At the start of a lunar month, we will see a **new moon**. Or maybe we won't – the new moon is pretty much invisible. Sun, moon and earth are in a line, but the moon is between the sun and the earth, so the side of the moon facing us is unlit. Once in a while, the lining-up is so exact that the moon's shadow actually falls onto the earth and we get a solar eclipse (of which

---

* Not cheese.

more later). Over the next few days, a **crescent moon** appears – specifically, a **waxing crescent** moon. The moon looks like a thin sickle. Waxing means it's becoming bigger. That doesn't make much sense – maybe think of wax building up on the sides of a wine bottle with a candle stuck in it. You can see this phase all through the daytime.

As the moon carries on, the sun catches more of its surface and by day seven of the lunar month we have a **waxing quarter moon**, then a **waxing half moon**. Onwards to day ten and the moon is more than half lit, and is rising ever later in the daytime and remaining on view into the night. When the moon passes the halfway point, it becomes a **gibbous moon** – in this case a **waxing gibbous moon**. The side that was first lit up is full and round, the other side grades into shadow close to the edge. On day fourteen the whole face of the moon visible from earth is lit – a **full moon,** which rises at sunset and sets at sunrise. Again, the sun, moon and earth are in a line, but now we are in the middle of the line. If the geometry is exactly lined up, the earth's shadow falls on the moon and produces a lunar eclipse, just as with the solar eclipse. A full moon in September is sometimes called a 'harvest moon'.

The process then happens in reverse – gibbous to half to quarter to crescent. When the amount of moon visible is becoming smaller, it's **waning**. No handy mental image needed to remind us of that. So we have a **waning gibbous moon, waning half moon, waning quarter moon** and **waning crescent moon** (all rising progressively later through the night), then finally back to new moon again. If you are in the northern hemisphere, you'll see the right edge of the moon light up first; in the southern hemisphere it's the other way round.

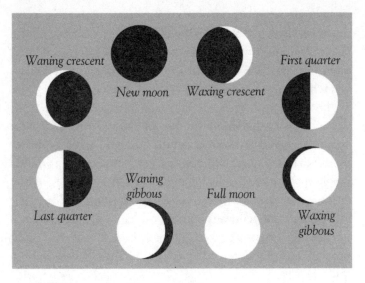

The phases of the moon

The moon and the tides

The moon is big enough and close enough to earth to exert a **gravitational pull**.* It isn't strong enough for moon and earth to hurtle towards each other and crash, but the moon's pull does affect some of the oceans on earth, causing tides.

The gravitational attraction of the moon causes the oceans to bulge out towards the moon, on the side of earth that's closest to the moon. Because of the earth's spin, an equivalent bulge forms on the opposite side. Think of two people holding hands and spinning in a circle: centrifugal force pulls them

---

* This isn't a physics book so here's a very brief explanation of gravity: it's the force that pulls solid objects towards each other. The bigger the object, the stronger the pull.

away from each other. Since earth is turning all the time while this is happening, the bulge moves around the earth, and the result is tides – two of them every twenty-four hours and fifty minutes (that's why the time of the tides changes day by day, and why we need tide tables).

The tides are biggest at the times of new moon and full moon, because that's when the moon is closest to us. This is actually because at these times the sun is lined up with the moon, so the gravity of both the sun and moon is pulling our seas in the same direction. These tides are called 'spring tides', but that's an analogy to a spring of water, nothing to do with the season. Tides during the quarter and half phases are smaller and are called 'neap tides'.*

The sun

Our sun is a star. In the scheme of things it's not an exceptionally big, hot or exciting star – it's classified as a **'yellow dwarf'** – but it would still be a mistake to fly a balloon into the heart of it, or even to stare at it with the naked eye.**
It is, of course, much bigger than earth or the other planets, and so its gravity pulls us and them around in our orbits.

Stars are made mostly of hydrogen, and are constantly burning, using up that hydrogen through **thermonuclear fusion** – a process which turns hydrogen into other, heavier elements and lets loose lots of heat. It will eventually use up

---

* 'Neap' is the pole of a horse-drawn cart, and also the name of a Scottish village. No idea what it has to do with tides.
** Most stars are dwarfs. Yellow dwarfs are actually bigger than red, white or brown ones.

all its hydrogen, and expand into a **red giant**. This may or may not consume the earth, but will certainly destroy all life on earth. So we will need to find a new place to live if we plan on sticking around longer than 5 billion more years.

For now, the sun is what keeps us alive. Its light drives photosynthesis in plants, and without plants there could be no animals. The fact that our nearest planet neighbours, Venus (nearer the sun than us) and Mars (further away) seem bereft of life suggests that life can't spring up on any old planet – distance from the sun is important.

Eclipses

Among the most wonderful things we can see from earth are solar eclipses, which occur when the path of the new moon takes it across the face of the sun. From where we are, the two discs look about the same size, so in a full solar eclipse the moon can completely mask the face of the sun, causing the sky to darken in daytime and a generally strange and spooky atmosphere to develop. The sudden falling of darkness in the middle of the day can be as confusing for animals as it is fascinating for us. Many observers have reported seeing birds heading off to roost during an eclipse, only to have to get up again a few minutes later.

There are up to two full solar eclipses a year, and a few more partial ones in which it looks like some celestial being has taken a bite out of the size of the sun. Each full eclipse is only visible from a relatively small area of the world, and so keen eclipse-spotters make long pilgrimages to see them.*

---

* And desperately hope it's not a cloudy day.

LEARN YOUR PLANETS

Most of us can name most of the planets, but getting them in the right order is a bit more challenging. Inevitably, bright sparks through the years have come up with mnemonics to help remember the order, which is:

Mercury

Venus

Earth

Mars

Jupiter

Saturn

Uranus

Neptune

Unfortunately, some of the mnemonics were devised when Pluto was still a planet, and don't make sense without it – e.g. 'My Very Easy Method – Just Set Up Nine Planets', or 'My Very Educated Mother Just Served Us Nine Pizzas'.

In 2006 *Astromony* magazine launched a competition to devise the best eight-planet mnemonic. The winner was 'My Violent Evil Monster Just Scared Us Nuts' from Kyle S. of Mississippi. Catchy.

Lunar eclipses occur when the earth's shadow falls on the moon. They are less spectacular, as there's no sky-darkening effect, but the moon goes an interesting, sometimes quite bright red-brown colour as the shadow spreads across it.

The planets

Our solar system contains eight planets (since Pluto was officially demoted to a 'dwarf planet', one of several, in 2006). The four inner planets are solid and rocky, the four outer ones are much bigger and mainly made of gas – hence their nickname the '**gas giants**'.

Seeing the planets isn't as easy as seeing the sun or the moon. You'll need a telescope or at least a decent pair of binoculars, and you'll need to use star charts to figure out where they'll be in the sky (some or all will be out of view at any given time). Venus is the brightest planet, brighter in fact than anything else in the sky save the sun and moon, and if you know what you're looking for you can find it with the naked eye, but through a telescope it is disappointing, any surface detail masked by the thick, gassy atmosphere.

Saturn and Jupiter take more finding, but through a good telescope are fantastic to look at. Jupiter is just behind Venus in terms of brightness and its banded yellow and red pattern, including the **Great Red Spot**, can easily be seen through a telescope, as can the ice-crystal rings of Saturn. Mars varies in brightness but often has a reddish glow that you can see with the naked eye. Mercury is too near the sun to be easily viewable, though you can find it at dusk or dawn. Of the outermost planets, Uranus can be seen with the naked eye but is difficult to recognize as a planet, and to see Neptune at all you'll need a telescope.*

---

* I must admit I typed and deleted a poor-taste Uranus joke here. No, you don't want to know.

PLANETARY PROPERTIES

The rocky planets have a core of mainly molten iron, covered over with a mantle of rock. The innermost two rocky planets have nothing orbiting them and Mercury has practically no atmosphere either. Venus has lots of atmosphere, but it's not a party atmosphere, it's a very dense one made mostly of carbon dioxide which helps keep the planet's surface a toasty 400°C. Mars has a thin atmosphere, which means its surface temperature fluctuates a great deal – from 20°C to minus 140°C. Mars has a couple of satellites – Phobos and Deimos. Both of these wonky-shaped bodies are too small to warrant being called moons.

Heading out to the gas giants, the hot and stormy gas ball Jupiter has an impressive collection of sixty-three satellites, a few of which (Ganymede, Callisto, Io and Europa) are similar to the rocky planets and offer probably the best chance of holding life in our solar system beyond earth. Saturn has sixty known satellites, one of which (Titan) is bigger than Mercury.

Uranus and Neptune have twenty-seven and thirteen satellites respectively. Neptune's largest moon, Triton, is geologically active, firing geysers of nitrogen into space. Both of these planets have rings of ice crystals like Saturn, but theirs are much less substantial. Uranus is the smallest and coldest gas giant.

Other night sky stuff

If you've always thought that shooting stars were actual stars falling from the heavens, it's time to stop worrying. They're **meteors**, flying lumps of rock that create a fiery trail when they enter earth's atmosphere. The friction of rapidly entering the atmospheric gases from the vacuum of space is what heats them up and sets them alight. Small ones are destroyed completely when this happens, but bits of the bigger ones may make it to earth. Very big meteors leave craters, and the arrival of a real whopper would cause the equivalent of a massive nuclear explosion. Many a thriller film has explored this possibility, and such 'impact events' are widely thought to be responsible for some major mass extinctions in earth's history. Actually, maybe it's not time to stop worrying.

Comets are flying rocky ice balls that orbit the sun, and some of them go past earth close enough for us to see them. Some trail a long 'tail' of dust. Our most famous comet is Halley's comet (I recommend you pronounce it 'Halley' to rhyme with 'valley' sound rather than 'Hayley') which comes around every seventy-five years or so. If you're still here in 2061 you could see it. The most dramatic comet of recent years was Comet Hale-Bopp, which lit up our skies for weeks in 1997. Sadly, it won't be back until 4530.

The stars we see at night are a mixture of the close-ish and the very far away, the big and the small. We like to play join-the-dots and give names to groups of stars that for us form consistent shapes, although these **constellations** are meaningless in terms of the stars' real positions. Nevertheless, it's fun and easy to learn constellations with the help of star charts, which show you what's on view from where you are at any given time. Orion and the Great Bear (aka the Plough or Ursa Major) are good starting points. You can see plenty with the naked eye, but a telescope really brings the night sky to life. If you've had a lousy day at work, there's nothing like a few hours staring into the cosmos to make it all seem less important.

Recommended reading

The Blind Watchmaker by Richard Dawkins. All about evolution and how it works. Dawkins's other books explore aspects of the same subject – *The Selfish Gene*, *Climbing Mount Improbable* and *Unweaving the Rainbow* all come highly recommended.

Wonderful Life by Stephen Jay Gould. A rather different evolution book, this looks at the fossils left behind from the 'Cambrian Explosion', when many modern life forms came into being for the first time. Also seek out Gould's collections of essays, with titles like *The Panda's Thumb*.

Guide to the Night Sky by Patrick Moore. One of more than seventy books on astronomy by the much-loved, monocled Moore, this will help you find and name constellations and other night-sky objects.

Collins Complete Guide to British Wildlife by Paul Sterry. If you only buy one identification or field guide, you'd probably best make it this one or one like it, as it covers everything from trees to toadstools and bats to beetles. There are many, many more field guides around, most of them sticking to smaller groupings of animals or plants.

Fauna Britannica by Stefan Buczacki and *Flora Britannica* by Richard Mabey. Two hefty volumes, dealing with animals and plants respectively. They're not identification guides, but are proper in-depth explorations of the history, biology and ecology of British wildlife. Both are full of information and lovely photos.

Index

References in *italics* refer to illustrations

sea urchins 151
seals 73, *73*
sedges 45–6
sedimentary rocks 172
seeds 16, 21–3, 42, 46
self-seeding 42
sharks 127
shellfish 150
shrews 65
shrubs 25, 29
silver birches 27
Sitka spruces *19*, 28
snakes 112–17, *111, 117*
snorkelling 136, 150
sparrowhawks 103, 109, 156, *157*
spawning 120–2, *122*, 133–4
species 128
spiders 148–9
sponges 151
spores 52
stamens 20, 38, *38*
starfish 151
stars 184–5
sticklebacks 135–6, *135*
stigma 20, 21, 36–7, *37*
stoats 65, 66, 67, 76, 161
sun 179–81
sundews 45
sunflowers 47
swans 108, 160
sycamores 21, 27

tadpoles 121–2, *122*, 123
taxonomies 128–9
tectonic plates 170, 173
thermonuclear fusion 179
thrushes 94, 158
tides 178–9
tits 94, 103, 105

toads 118–19, 120, 121, 123
toadstools 50, 52, 53
trees 15–31; bark 18; berries 23–4;
     deciduous 17, 20; embryos 19;
     evergreen 17–20; gametes 19;
     leaves 25, *29–30*; species of
     26–9; wood 18
troposphere 166
tsunamis 173

ultraviolet light 34, 39
umbellifers 44
ungulates 63
Uranus 181, 182, 183

Venus 180, 181, 182, 183
volcanoes 170–3, *171*, 173

waders 89
warblers 94–5, *100*
'warning colouration' 159
wasps 140, 146
water vapour 166–7, 168
waterfowl 89
weasels 65, 67, 76
weather 166–70
whales 74
wind 168–9
wolf spiders 149
wood 18
woodpeckers 97
worms 151
wrens 95–6

yellow dwarfs 179
yews 27

zebra spiders 149